No Longer Afraid

By Donna M. Cox
PBM Press 2010
All Rights Reserved

Published in 2010 in the United States of America by Personal Best Ministries Press/Donna Cox Ministries, a subsidiary of Personal Best Ministries LLC, 211 Stratford Lane, Xenia, Ohio 45385.

Library of Congress Cataloging-in-Publication Data
Cox, Donna M.
No Longer Afraid: Breaking Free of the Fear That Has You Bound /Donna Cox

     ISBN 978-0-9796955-2-0
     Includes poetry
     Includes bibliographic references
     Includes biblical quotations and references
     Includes photographs
     Includes illustrations
     Religious subtext

For speaking engagements, you may contact the author at:
Rev. Dr. Donna M. Cox
Personal Best Ministries LLC
Email: revdonna.cox@gmail.com
Website: http://revdonc.wordpress.com

A 2010 Publication of *Donna Cox Ministries*
A subsidiary of

PERSONAL
BEST
MINISTRIES

Foreword by Lisa Strauther McNeal

I admit it. I am addicted to worry, and they say that admitting you have a problem is the first step to recovery. I am an expert in the art of "what ifs" and "if onlys." Not only that, but I am very proficient at worrying for others as well. I worry for my children, my siblings, my friends, even my husband.

Sadly, I seem to have passed this gift to my son either by example or through DNA. Last week while studying for a spelling bee, my son became anxiety ridden over the possibility that he was not fully prepared. In fact, no amount of studying would have eased his worry. So, I had him reading scripture to reinforce God's desire for us concerning worry, fear and anxiety. At this point my ten year–old daughter made a monumental statement. She said, "You know Mom, we learned in religion that worry is a sin against God." Wow, I was floored. This is something I know in my head, but have not truly hidden in my heart that I might not sin against Him.

In *No Longer Afraid*, Dr. Cox effectively lays out the issues, obstacles and consequences that occur when we let fear, worry and anxiety get a foothold in our minds. The enemy sends fear to render believers powerless. Dr. Cox shows us that, like an out–of–control snowball rolling down a hill, worry can overpower even the best of us, spiritually and physically. 1 John 4:18 says: "There is no fear in love. But perfect loves drives out fear, because fear has to do with punishment. The one who fears is not made perfect in love." We know that this perfect love is God, and if we abide in this love, can there be fear?

If you desire to break free from the bondage of worry, fear and anxiety; if you are courageous enough to examine yourself and your fears, and confront them head on, come with me on a journey through this insightful book. God desires you to be free, to live an abundant life, to walk in faith not fear, and to stay focused on Him. Through this book, learn to harness the resurrection power of the Holy Spirit who dwells within you, power available to you this day. You will not be disappointed and you will be "No Longer Afraid."

This book is dedicated to:

✝ Gerald, my husband of nearly 29 years; the enemy is a liar! Thank you Honey for continuing to let God shape you into the awesome man He created you to be. Thank you for being the prayer warrior for our ministry!

✝ My son, Jonathan, who inspires me with his insightful and powerful poetry and songs. Jonathan, even though you've witnessed God ordering your steps in miraculous ways, your eyes still haven't seen, your ears haven't heard, nor have you begun to imagine all God will do in your life. I can hardly wait to see it myself!

✝ My daughter, Jamie, whose beautiful photography and artwork decorate our world. Jamie, from the moment you were a small girl I knew God had gifted you for an awesome purpose. Remember, God is faithful and will complete the great work He has already begun in you. Open your heart and soar! I'll be watching with great anticipation and joy.

✝ Hezekiah, my darling grandson, who always makes me laugh and reminds me there is reason to hope and trust in the Lord. I look forward to seeing the many ways God will bless the world through the talents and caring spirit I already see in you.

✝ My Lord and Savior who knows everything there is to know about me and *despite my shortcomings*, still called me into the ministry. It is my heartfelt desire to worship and serve You with integrity, passion, creativity, intelligence and obedience. Jesus, make me more like You every day!

Acknowledgements:
Special thanks to the ladies who participated in the home Bible study that served as the basis for this book. You helped me flesh out concepts but more importantly, you allowed me to be faithful and obedient to the Lord. It would be difficult for me to get a book to print without Lisa who functions as reader/editor. Her comments and insight are always appreciated and force me to go deeper. Likewise, my brother Danny takes time from his busy schedule to read, offer comments and press me to greater clarity about my ideas and concepts. My cousin, LeShawn responded immediately to my request for a cover design and began the process of matching his talents with my vision. I enjoyed working with illustrator, Marilyn, though we've never met. What a gift she has and is! I look forward to future collaborations. I must also thank the following for unqualified support that makes it possible to keep walking in the anointing and call God placed on my life: the wonderful, awesome people in my Marriage Builders Sunday School class; Daria with whom I can share anything; the members of our Covenant Group – Diana & Joe, John & Rexann, Terry & Sylvia; Mom & Dad Cox, my biggest fans and supporters; Marshielle and Katrina, the best sisters a girl can have; and adopted niece, Lori my personal marketing expert who loves and covers me with daily prayer.

Table of Contents

Section One
Owning The Problem
6

Section Two
Defining The Enemy
23

Section Three
Walking The Talk
60

ʟ

Part 1
Owning The Problem

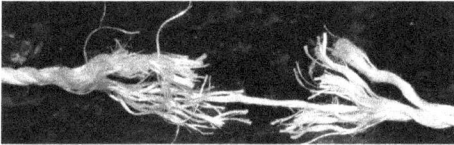

7

Search me, O God,
and know my heart;
Test me and know my anxious thoughts
Psalm 139:23 NLT

1
An Attitude? Who, Me?

"To be wronged is nothing unless you continue to remember it." Unknown

I was driving through the streets of Dayton one fine day in the late fall when I had an epiphany; I have an attitude problem! The revelation that I had an attitude problem was in no way related to what folk may perceive about the quirks of my personality. In fact, the revelation was not at all about my personality. God was speaking directly to my heart about the ways I have allowed thoughts to control my life. My *undisciplined mind* was the problem. I could easily borrow the words of the apostle Paul and say 'the things I should think, I don't. The things I don't want to think, I do. Oh wretched woman am I!'[1] My attitude problem kept me awake at night, worrying and replaying conversations I had already had, wished I had, should have had and likely never would have. Certainly, there was little likelihood I would have had any of these conversations at 3:00 a.m. in the morning!

In truth, this light-bulb moment should not have surprised me. I've had an attitude problem most of my life. And it has caused me to spend far too much of my precious life living in fear. I didn't often admit to being afraid. In fact, to most people I usually appeared extremely confident and competent. Not many people knew I waited for the bottom to drop out of my world. Few would have believed I often thought of myself as stupid and incompetent. I lived in a constant state of anxiety. The truth is that sometimes even *I* didn't realize I lived this way. All I really knew was how often I felt misunderstood, disheartened, discouraged and

---

[1] Paraphrase of Romans 7:15

9

alone. When I was Chair of the Department of Music on the campus where I work, I genuinely wanted my colleagues to like me. At the same time I needed them to respect me and I often had to make unpopular decisions or have difficult conversations - sometimes with people I had once considered friends. I wanted my children to adore me but I was often hard on them, not because they were bad children but because of my fear of what *could* happen. I wanted my husband to treat me like a precious jewel but I was often prickly and difficult to get along with. When you live your life like this, you act like Dr. Jekkle and Mr. Hyde and confuse people most of the time. When your mind is undisciplined, your attitude and actions change from one minute to the next, often giving people around you emotional and mental whiplash in the process.

Coupled with fear and anxiety was a constant state of worry. I half-heartedly joked with people that one of my gifts was worry. If there was something that could be worried about, I worried. Certainly, as I was growing up, I had many reasons to worry. I was raised by my maternal grandmother in an abusive, alcoholic environment. Not only was my home-life unstable, my life was sometimes threatened. Rather than dealing with the residue of this harmful upbringing, I mentally "divorced" myself from my past and attempted to move forward. Since I made this decision in secret there was no one to help me to understand the impossibility of divorcing your past. It took many years for me to realize that the only way *out* is to be willing to go *through*. This means going back and dealing with issues, not in one's own strength but with the power of the Lord.

As a minister of the gospel I've known for a long time what and how I *should* think. I also knew how to *talk* about how and what I *should* be thinking. I had read the books. I had even taught the classes. Since I'm a crafter, I had even made the tee shirts! I wasn't being fraudulent; I truly believed the things I read and taught. At the same time, I was not living in total victory. Once, I tried to confess this to one of my closest friends. She brushed off my concerns and reminded me that worry was unbiblical! Since I already knew that, I laughed it off and left the conversation feeling even more condemned. I wished it were as easy for me to stop worrying as she made it seem. I would lay in bed ruminating over some problem I was having with a co-worker. In my mind I would say to her all of the things I didn't say during the day. All of the witty, and if I'm honest, *cutting* comebacks that I had not said during the day would roll around in my mind. Or I would lay in bed worrying about whether or not I would get a good evaluation. Would I be able to maintain my job? Would a negative evaluation shout to the world I was worthless? Would the pastor ever recognize the care that I put into the ministry I led and finally agree to ordain me? I would worry about not being able to pay the bills even though we made very good salaries. I'd worry that my son, whom I had had to correct for overspending his budget, would stop loving me for doing so. Negative thoughts and nagging worry would wake me from a deep sleep. During that time of the night when your spirit is so open, I would lie awake fretting.

I tried to pray but the words would get all mixed up with the conversations going on in my mind. I had read somewhere in one of the hundreds of self-help books lining my bookshelves that meditating on the word would chase away these negative thoughts. It seemed like a simple formula. That too seemed to fail me at times and I would end up, not only having spent an hour or two meditating on the *wrong things*, but also laden with guilt that I was a failure in this area of my life. Where was God in the middle of the night when the battle was raging in my mind *and I was losing?* And as I was crying out to the Lord for deliverance – for *real* this time - from fear

11

and anxiety, God planted this book in my spirit. God showed me that I am *empowered* to make lasting changes in my attitude.

Attitudes affect the actions we take in every area of our lives. Like many people, the lack of discipline in my attitude has been manifested in a constant struggle with my weight. Over the years I have tried every diet I could find to get the extra pounds that seemed to increase with each new decade off my frame. And invariably, I would fail at every one. It occurred to me I was always looking for a quick fix to a long-term problem. I wanted the microwave fix. I tried to eat cabbage soup for two weeks. I lasted two days. I tried Weight Watchers™ until I realized I was routinely eating six two-point bars™ and two bags of popcorn. I wasn't losing weight nor was I eating a healthy meal. I tried Adkins™ but the idea of giving up popcorn and pizza seemed nearly impossible to me. I tried the protein power diet and the carbohydrate addicts diet. I bought some pills from an infomercial that promised to magically cure my eating issues. I tried a patch that was going to curb my appetite. I tried pills that were going to flush the toxins from my system and help me shed nine pounds of waste the manufacturer said I was carrying in my body. I'd be successful for a short time but then I'd find myself falling easily back into old habits. It would start simply enough. I'd decide that eating this one little thing- this *time* - wasn't going to hurt. And before I knew it, I had gotten away from whatever good habits I was trying to develop.

Finally, I realized I had to change my attitude about food and eating. I had to accept that there were foods I needed to avoid as much as possible. I had to look in the mirror and see a middle-aged woman and not the svelte cheerleader I had once been. I told myself if I wanted to be healthier and slimmer, I was going to have to let some of that stuff go. Bit by bit, I began to change the way I thought about food. I decided to rid myself of the attitude that foods were *bad* and begin to consider that some foods were simply *better* for me than others. Thus began a new, more disciplined way of thinking and eating.

Shaping a better attitude about food is a metaphor for what it takes to make any lasting change. As I changed my eating and began to lose pounds that always seem to find me every time I lost them, God revealed several truths to me. I had tried several times to lose weight. I kept copious records. I kept the goals I had established for myself. On one particular goal sheet I had scratched off starting dates and written new ones *four times*! God revealed that I was neither helping change my attitudes nor ensuring a positive outcome. I was actually keeping a record of my *failures*! This was not God's idea! Only Satan would want me to remember the many times I had started and failed! Only the adversary would want to keep me locked in the old attitude. I was attempting to start something *new* already shackled by the *old*. Jesus taught a similar principle. He said, *"No one sews a patch of unshrunk cloth on an old garment, for the patch will pull away from the garment, making the tear worse. Neither do men pour new wine into old wineskins. If they do, the skins will burst, the wine will run out and the wineskins will be ruined. No, they pour new wine into new wineskins, and both are preserved."[2]*

I needed a new attitude. As a result, I had to throw away every record of a failed plan. I threw away the records of my recycled intentions to be and eat healthier. I threw away the photos I had taken, the ones that were going to be the *before* picture to the some-day-in-the-future *after* picture. I didn't need to be reminded of how many times over the past ten years I had tried (and failed) to lose weight. With my new

---

[2] Matthew 9:16-17

attitude, I could practice the scriptural principles I already knew. I could speak those things that were not as though they were. I *could* be successful this time. I *would* be successful this time. But, I would have to do a new thing. Losing weight meant adjusting wrong attitudes and disciplining my flesh, not just for the time that it would take to get the weight under control, but for the rest of my life.

I also had to recognize that a new attitude had to come from within. Anyone who has begun a diet program understands fairly early that people are not predisposed to helping you reach that goal. There are always people who will tell you that you don't need to lose weight. This is especially true for people who are only a few pounds overweight. People constantly say you look fine and should enjoy life! They sabotage your efforts by offering you the very things you have already determined not to eat. When you try to stand firm, they tease you about your discipline. The old adage that misery loves company is especially true when you become serious about changing your life. Most people don't want you to eat right, think right, or be right because it makes them feel guilty about their own lack of discipline. A big step in changing any bad attitude about food is learning not to let people coheres you into making wrong decisions. Ultimately, *you* are responsible for what you put inside your body. *You* are responsible for your own thoughts and actions. Likewise, when you begin to shake off other weights, people will work against your efforts. Therefore, it is crucial that you are convinced in your own heart and resolute in your own mind.

Living a life shackled by the weights of fear, worry and anxiety has mirrored my ever-present struggle with food. I've kept copious records of all of my worries and fears in prayer journal after prayer journal. Pouring out my fear and anxiety to God is a good thing. That's not the problem. God cares and wants us to cast all of our cares on Him. The problem comes when you pour out all the cares and then scoop them back up! Clearly, I needed a new attitude, not just about food, but about *all* areas of my life. On that fall afternoon when the Lord spoke to me about my attitude problem, I recalled many scriptures where God issues imperatives: do not fear; do not be anxious; don't let your heart be troubled. In my car I had another epiphany; if God said *don't*, it's because I have the power *not to*. How liberating! God will never tell me to do something if it is not within my ability to accomplish the task. If I have problems accomplishing a task, be it eating a sensible diet, speaking kindly, or sleeping instead of worrying, the answer is in the way I *choose* to look at and approach the task.

Being obedient to God's imperatives requires two things: First, there has to be an underlying faith that the task can be done. Second, the requisite action must follow. When Peter asked Jesus to let him come to him on the water, Peter had to start with the faith that he could actually do it. However, faith alone was not enough. Peter had to actually *get out of the boat* and *start walking*. Peter had the faith to get out of the boat. He even took a few steps. Then he allowed the things he could see (water, lots and lots of water) and his own understanding (Peter knew people didn't walk on water) stop his forward action.[3] How many times have I, like Peter, been guilty of this? How many times have I allowed past experiences and present situations to determine my attitude and thwart the positive future God promises? It has happened more times than I care to recall. But on that day in my car, I felt a new sense of hope well up in my spirit. This time would be different! Like pop theologian, Patti LaBelle, I began to sing a new song.

---

[3] Matthew 14:22-31

15

*Running hot, running cold, I was running into
overload. It was extreme. I took it so high,
so low, so low there was nowhere to go like
a bad dream. Somehow the wires uncrossed,
the tables were turned, never knew I had such
a lesson to learn. I'm feeling good from my
head to my shoes, know where I'm going and
I know what to do. I tidied up my point of view.
I got a new attitude.*[4]

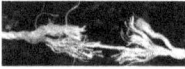

Shredding The Cord:

The faith walk is constantly about putting action to the things you say you believe. Identify at least one area where this seems to be a constant struggle for you.

How can you move more quickly from faith to action? Commit to taking one faith move this week!

---

[4] Composed by Sharon Robinson, Jon Gilutin and Bunny Hull

2
I Don't Think So

"Nothing in the affairs of men is worthy of great anxiety." Plato

Being victorious in any area of your life requires discipline and tenacity. Using what I learned from my constant struggle with eating as a way of thinking about other areas of my life was liberating. I developed skills that would make serving God easier and my spiritual walk more victorious. Once I figured I had gotten it together, I was ready to transfer these new skills to an area of my life that seemed to be spiraling out of control- fear and anxiety.

It is no coincidence that as soon as I committed to applying what I was learning, Satan launched a series of major attacks on my life. I started the fall semester determined to walk in full victory. My tenure as Department Chair had been fraught with tension as certain people challenged my leadership. I typically internalized every complaint and criticism. The prior semester I had undergone a very painful evaluation before being reappointed for another four-year term. Although I had not emerged from the evaluation unscathed, I did emerge victorious. God proved that man does not have the power or authority to shut any door God opens. I knew God had placed me as Chair and I was determined to lay aside the weight of the position and enjoy the journey. We were not one week into the semester before I became embroiled in a misunderstanding with my Dean, not a comfortable place to find oneself under the best of circumstances. Every year at the beginning of the semester I hosted an event designed to build community between new and returning students and the faculty. This was a long-standing tradition, even prior to my administration. This year, our Dean scheduled a workshop for the same time. Dutifully, I followed what had been standard protocol. I sent an email explaining why I would be absent from the workshop and proceeded with planning the Department gathering. That simple email launched a series of events that were shocking and disturbing. Needless to say I cancelled our Department event and took myself to the Dean's. I was angry and confused. First, I believed strongly in the importance of our annual Department gathering and thought it should have had priority. Second, I knew several Chairs who were not attending the workshop and who had not bothered to explain their absences. Finally, the workshop was on diversity, an issue in which I had been intimately involved since my arrival on campus. Yet, I was made to feel as if not attending signaled a lack of commitment and a dismissal all of the years of work I had done on campus.

   None of what I have articulated here was told to the Dean, of course. I talked to my husband about it and internalized much of what I felt. I began to fear the Dean's opinion of me. I worried about the negative impact this exchange might have on my ability to lead our department. I worried that future raises would be diminished. If a problem could be connected to this event, the thoughts plagued me. Yet, I didn't suspect any of this was having a negative impact on my body. A month into school my acid reflux kicked into high gear. There seemed to be something lodged in my throat and I tried everything I could to get it to move. When self-medication didn't work, I went to see my primary care physician who prescribed acid medicines and an appointment with a gastroenterologist. Dr. E, a wonderfully calm woman, performed her exam then quietly asked if I were under a lot of stress. As it turned out, my reflux was actually mild but my anxiety was high. I was diagnosed with globus hystericus, a disease common among type A people.[5] I left her office, not with acid medicine but with a prescription for an antidepressant! Later, my TMJ[6] began to worsen and opening my mouth fully in the mornings became nearly impossible. Sometimes, it would take the first thirty minutes of the morning before I could open wide enough to brush my teeth. A visit to the dentist and an expensive exam later confirmed Dr. E's diagnosis; I was seriously stressed and attempting to solve all of my problems while I slept.

As if the stress over my job were not enough, my resolve to walk in victory was further tested by the issue of ordination. The question of whether or not I would be ordained at my home church had been painful for quite some time. The pastor insisted I obtain some kind of master's degree in theology, preferably a Masters of Divinity even though I already possessed bachelors, masters and doctoral degrees and had taken several graduate courses in religious studies. I found it difficult to understand the rationale when I saw others ordained without meeting that stipulation. I didn't have a problem with those who had been ordained. I honestly supported their ministries. I was merely hurt and confused about why *I* hadn't been ordained. The idea that I might need to find another church was devastating. The stress load got heavier.[7]

---

[5] Globus Hystericus is the sensation of a lump in the throat with difficulty swallowing and no physical cause. For many, stress is the underlying cause.

[6] The Temporo-Mandibular Joint (TMJ) is the one immediately in front of the ear on each side of your head and is one of the most frequently used of all joints of the body. TMJ dysfunction is often aggravated by high levels of personal stress.

[7] I completed the Masters in Theological Studies in May 2008 and was ordained on April 19, 2009 by the American Baptist Churches USA at my home church. I praise God for not allowing my anger and pain to short-circuit His best plan for my life. I

I had obviously not stopped fear at the door but had given it and its two best friends, worry and anxiety, full access to my life. And my body was screaming at me to kick them out. I pressed through the academic year, teaching my home study on fear and believing I was making strides. However, Satan was not through testing my intentions to live victoriously. Because of my own traumatic and dysfunctional childhood, family is very important in my life. Although my husband and I had not always shared a warm and fuzzy relationship, I believed we were fully committed to each other and that we would be married forever. I had been teaching a Sunday school class for married couples for several years. I had also organized and taught many marriage retreats and workshops. God had given me a measure of success with couples that were going through problems. It never really occurred to me that my husband might not be as fully committed as I. Overnight, my entire world turned upside down and it appeared that fear and anxiety would be permanent residents in my life. I teetered on the brink of full collapse under the weight. For a moment I questioned God's call on my life. How could I teach other couples if my own marriage was dead? How could I talk about victory when I felt like such a failure? Slowly, God began to pull me out of the maelstrom. I pressed on.

When I thought the dust had finally settled and things were under control, Satan launched one more attack. Late one afternoon my daughter asked me to stay at the office so we could talk. She had also asked her Dad to join us. When we had assembled, she told us she was pregnant. We had been working so hard to keep her in school, to encourage her to take advantage of the opportunity to earn her degree. Satan was

---

continue to learn that God's timing is not mine and doors that seem to be shut by man may very well be God's way of saying 'wait!"

convinced his strategies had won the war. Satan called his party planner and ordered a full celebration. He was excited to think he had destroyed my marriage, my self-esteem, my child and her future. He thought he had taken my ministry. He thought he was going to sidetrack me and leave me lying in my bed weighted by the spirit of depression. However, Satan was sorely mistaken! God gave me a great sense of peace, the kind of peace that makes no sense in the natural realm. Instead of worrying about all of the challenges my daughter would face as a single Mom who had yet to complete her college education; instead of thinking too deeply about how *her* decision would impact *my life*, I thanked God she didn't have a terminal disease. I thanked God for the resources to help her through the pregnancy and completion of her degree.

Satan was shocked to see me picking up the draft of this book, determined to complete it and get it into the hands of others he thought he had also destroyed. Satan was appalled to discover my husband and I considered our soon-to-be-born grandchild a blessing not one of the enemy's tools for destruction. Satan got a kick in the face when he discovered that, although our marriage was seriously broken, it was definitely not beyond repair. What the enemy meant for evil, God would use for good. Satan had to call his minions to tell them the party had been cancelled! Instead of being broken under the weights the enemy had piled on, God gave me hope and a renewed purpose. As you read this book and internalize the teachings, I fully expect you to tell Satan to cancel the party he has planned over your life.

Shredding The Cord:

Identify one or two struggles in your life where the enemy may think he's going to win.

Redirect your thoughts. Celebrate the fact that if the enemy *could have* defeated you, he would have already done so! Thank God **now** for the victory you have yet to see! Put your words of praise and thanksgiving in writing, either on this page or on another to hang in your kitchen or bathroom.

Part 2:
Defining The Enemy

How long will my enemy be exalted over me?
Psalm 13:2b

3
Fear: False Evidence Appearing Real....
And Causing Problems

"I believe that anyone can conquer fear by doing the things he fears to do,
provided he keeps doing them until he gets a record of successful
experiences behind him." Eleanor Roosevelt
"Heavy thoughts bring on physical maladies; when the soul is
oppressed so is the body." Martin Luther

For much of my life I would have vehemently denied, even to myself, that I was saddled with fear. My childhood was fraught with the intense emotions associated with the trauma of living in an alcoholic family. I knew my history had created issues that followed me for years into my future. I would admit (sheepishly) that there were times in my adult life when I might have still been a bit anxious about spending the night alone in our house. At the same time, I could justify those feelings since our huge house was in a fine neighborhood bordered by less-desirable communities. I had spent my adulthood creating a life quite different from the childhood I had known. It never occurred to me that fear could lie seething under the surface. I never suspected that fear could and would manifest itself in ways totally unrelated to fear of the dark or things that go bump in the night. Several years ago I attended a leadership training session designed to help people manage their own success. The leader explained that our interpersonal reactions and interactions come from two opposing perspectives: hurt and worth. In practically every example she gave, I saw my own actions in the light of truth and I felt exposed and vulnerable. I sat in the room, trying to look like a professional while inside I wanted to sob. I discovered that most of my reactions - to my colleagues, children, and husband, even my pastor - were hurt-based!

Hurt-based responses and reactions are motivated by a fear of loss; *Will people dislike me if I make this decision? Will I lose the support of people I've thought of as friends if I take a different stand on an issue?* Hurt-based communicators often feel anger, hostility, anxiety, emptiness, rejection, confused and inadequate. Their own fears give birth to individual isolation, disrespect, confusion, and repressed feelings of inadequacy. And as a result, fearful people often respond forcefully and angrily or at the other extreme, they become doormats, letting people walk all over them while seething on the inside. The underlying, unspoken assumption that you *become* your mistakes can be paralyzing. Hurt-based responses are rooted in the belief that making wrong decisions lowers your value as a person. These responses say you are a failure if you make people angry. They convince you that *what you do* is more important than *who you are*. That belief creates tremendous internal pressure. Hurt-based reactions feed upon themselves and create a downward spiral of ungodly responses.

On the other hand, worth-based responses are centered in the realization that, *at the core*, you are a person of value. You may sometimes make bad decisions but doing so does not make you less valuable. You have inherent value that has *nothing* to do with how others perceive you. Your value is not contingent upon how much money you have, how many degrees you possess or any other temporal situation. Worth-based perspectives give you permission to be human, to make a mistake, pick yourself up and move forward. Being rooted and grounded in a worth-based philosophy helps you see your colleagues, family and friends for their inherent value, regardless of how they are acting at any given time. This philosophy is deeply rooted in Biblical values. God may not be pleased with your actions and attitudes at all times but God always loves you! God's actions illustrate how you are supposed to respond to others. Even though humankind had moved so far away from the ideal God established in the Garden of Eden, God still felt compassion and was moved to act. God sent Jesus as a sacrifice *because* you are a person of value. Living a worth-based life will help you be better parents, siblings, spouses, cousins, employers, whatever your shifting roles may be. When you acknowledge that the people with whom you interact on a daily basis were created in the very image of the triune God, it will free you from holding them to a standard they can't possibly reach. It frees you from holding yourself to that impossible standard as well.

What is fear?
Fear can be defined as an "emotional reaction characterized by unpleasant, often intense feelings, and by a desire to flee or hide."[8] It would be erroneous to say there is no value in fear. This emotion was created by God and has its uses. However, it is also a tool that Satan has perverted and uses effectively against us. "If fear has become commonplace, anxiety has become endemic," wrote David Wells in his book, *God in the Wasteland*.[9] This epidemic of fear has affected every level of our society. Childhood fears of insects, darkness, heights, being left alone, and of school give way to middle-age fears of unemployment, war, robbery, stock-market crashes, ill-health and our children going astray. These in turn give way to old-age fears of cancer, heart disease, technological change and death. Although the evidence Satan uses to convince us to be afraid is usually faulty, fear produces very real consequences.

---

[8] Schreur, Jack and Jerry, Family Fears: Overcoming the Worries That Threaten Our Families. Victor Books, 1994, page 19.
[9] Wells, David, God in the Wasteland: The Reality of Truth in a World of Fading Dreams, Eerdmans Publishing, 1994, page 97.

Psychologists describe three responses to fear: cognitive, emotional and physiological. Fear begins on a cognitive level, in the mind. When an outside stimulus is presented, the mind sends an immediate message in reaction. This message reports to the body that something bad is about to happen. At this point emotions take over and feelings of anxiety result. This anxiety can be either acute, as in the case of real, immediate danger or a general sense of angst that many people feel every day. Feelings of anxiety are the direct result of the stimuli sent by the brain. This emotional response then prompts the body to join the fray. Often there are accompanying physical responses such as a sudden tightness in the stomach, shortness of breath or other physical responses to the cognitive and emotional messages. The body is the last to get the news but it is not the silent partner. Many people are ill today because of the chemical baths that occur as the result of exposure to fear.

Norman Wright describes fear as a powerful negative drive that compels you forward while inhibiting your progress at the same time. Fear, like a hangman's noose, slowly tightens around your neck if you move in the wrong direction. Even when you are at the threshold of success, fear has the power to sabotage your best plans and efforts. Wright explains that fear is often the "unknown/unidentified motivator causing tension, disagreement and difficult relations." [10] It is an unseen yet extremely powerful force that must be acknowledge and resisted. Too often people refuse to see their actions as the result of their fears. When you refuse to acknowledge that fear is influencing you, the noose begins to tighten its grip on your life. And the result is not a pretty sight! Do you remember playing tug-a-war when you were a child? We used to play a version where two friends grabbed the hands of a third person.

[10] Ibid, page 21.

The goal for the center person was to stand her ground while the other two attempted to pull her to their side. When the two friends started pulling in opposite directions, the challenge began. At the point when it seemed as if one person would win, the other got another burst of energy and jerked the poor middle person back in the opposite direction. Fear is similar to tug-a-war but it is hardly a game! Fear propels you to move forward into some kind of positive action but there always seems to be a negative force yanking you back to the same place. Eventually, if the positive movement is counter-balanced with the same level of negative motion, you wear a rut in the ground!

Let's take a brief look at eight major problems associated with fear. Each of these issues will be explored in greater detail in subsequent chapters.

1. **Fear robs you of perspective.** It steals your peace of mind, shatters your self-esteem and strips you of confidence. It makes you overly cautious and afraid to make decisions. Fear diminishes your ability to achieve. Ultimately, fear derails you and robs you of the ability to reach your full potential in God.

2. **Fear diminishes God's role in your life.** When you let fear take charge, you tell God He is not big enough or does not care enough about your problems to handle them. There are more than 350 commandments to *fear-not* in the Bible and your ability to follow these commandments is dependant upon your ability to lean on and trust in God. As you will see throughout this

book, there is a strong connection between your trust in God and your ability to release fear and anxiety.

3. **Fear shifts your focus from God to yourself.** Fear makes you think you have to be in control of every situation in your life. Instead of surrendering control to a wise God who lovingly guides and cares for you, fear makes you act as if the weight of the entire world rests on your shoulders. You end up trying to juggle too many things and eventually they all come tumbling down.

4. **Fear causes anger.** At the root of many angry outbursts is fear. Fear of having a weakness exposed, of being invalidated, of being unloved, of losing a sense of power often hide behind the veneer of anger. Anger is a vicious and destructive cycle but many people prefer to deal with the negative results of anger rather than admit to being afraid.

5. **Fear makes you fight or flee.** Your body was designed with two responses when your mind senses danger: fight or flight. When true danger is present, one of these responses will be the correct one. On the other hand, many people live in the negative shadows of these two God-given responses. Some people choose to fight whenever they are fearful. This often leads to controlling behaviors. Some people elect to flee (physically or emotionally) rather than face the consequences of boldly confronting the object of their fear. Inappropriate flee or fight responses prevent believers from claiming God's promise of victory.

6. **Fear drives out peace.** In John 14: 27 Jesus states that the peace He leaves is unlike anything that the world knows and understands. Therefore, he says, "do not let your hearts be troubled and do not be afraid." Jesus was very intentional in the use of the words 'do not let'

because he wanted you to know that *you alone* have authority over your emotions. It should be abnormal for a Christian to live choked by fear and anxiety. Left unchecked, fear will drive out the peace that is your inheritance.

7. **Fear leads to destruction.** A fearful believer has no power against Satan who comes to steal, kill and destroy.[11] Satan is never satisfied until you are totally ineffective, inefficient or dead! Make no mistake, Satan is not Wile E. Coyote and you are not Sam, the sheepdog.[12] You are not playing a friendly game with Satan. There are no "do-overs" from his perspective. The enemy wants you counted out. But you have the power to resist the devil and put him to flight. Fear inhibits the ability to live the full, abundant, prosperous life that Jesus came to give.

8. **Fear makes you a minister of death.** You minister death by the words you speak. How many times do you say *innocent* things like "it almost scared me to death" or "I nearly lost my mind?" Careless conversation is never innocent to the enemy. You may think you do not mean anything by the words you speak but Satan is a legalist. He does not care what you *meant*. He only cares about what you *said*. Satan goes directly to what you *said* to contaminate your faith. Satan is always looking for an entry point into your life and fear is one of his most powerful tools. Satan uses fear to influence

---

[11] John 10:10

[12] WILE E. COYOTE was created by cartoon genius, Chuck Jones, at Warner Bros. Chuck Jones introduced Wile E. Coyote to the world in September 1949 in the Looney Tunes cartoon "Fast and Furry-ous". It would be three years, May 1952, before Road Runner would appear again with Wile E. Coyote in "BEEP, BEEP."

your mind, ideas, words, and actions. Fear will keep you from walking in the confidence of Christ.

Shredding The Cord:

Think carefully about a situation or person that consistently gets under your skin. Can you identify the 'fear factor' underlying your reactions? In what ways have you been using anger to cover fear?

How can you begin to transition from fear-based to worth-based reactions?

Think about the words you spoke today. Can you identify times careless words contaminated or had the potential to contaminate your faith?

4
Worry and Anxiety

"Do not anticipate trouble or worry about what may never happen.
Keep it in the sunlight." Benjamin Franklin
"Anxiety is a thin stream of fear trickling through the mind. If encouraged,
it cuts a channel into which all other thoughts are drained. "
Arthur Somers Roche
"Worry gives a small thing a big shadow" Swedish Proverb

I noticed my friend Maureen as soon as I walked into the conference room. She was sitting on the other side of the room, in conversation with Karen. As I made my way across the room intending to sit beside her, she looked up. I smiled broadly, prepared to give her one of our traditional quips. Instead of the warm, friendly smile I expected, she merely nodded and resumed talking. Karen didn't smile or nod. She simply glanced in my direction before looking back to Maureen. Arrested, I put my folder next to Charlie, grabbed a soft drink and sat down. I could barely keep my mind on the meeting I was so distracted by Maureen's behavior. I racked my brain for any clue to why she had given me the cold shoulder. Had I done something to offend her? I thought back over our conversations the past few days. I turned over every word looking for nuances I had obviously missed. Apparently, something was wrong since she couldn't even give me a decent smile. As I sat there, covertly watching Maureen, I imagined her telling Karen the many sins I had committed. Trying to maintain my composure, I joked with Charlie while my insides churned. Maureen and I were *friends*. Shouldn't she have told *me* if I had done something to offend her? Why did she have to wait until we were in a room full of colleagues to give me the cold shoulder? Everyone knew we were best friends; we sat together at every meeting. It must be obvious to all that something was drastically wrong. And since Maureen was the quieter of the two of us I was quite sure I would end up being the villain. The more I thought about it, the more my confusion mounted and the more agitated I felt inside. When the meeting adjourned I grabbed my folder and headed out the door. There was no way I was going to stay in the room and let the worry I felt show; I am absolutely no good at hiding my emotions.

For the rest of the day I ruminated. Hadn't she sounded strange when we talked yesterday? Was she telling me, in a not-so-subtle way, that she no longer wanted to be friends? This seemed silly and even childish to me but I couldn't seem to shake the thoughts. Maureen and I had been good friends for years. We had seen each other through some very difficult times and I didn't want to lose that. When Gerald got home I told him about Maureen's strange behavior. All of the anxiety I felt bubbled to the surface. In my telling, the nod she had given me seemed even more sinister. Everything about the day suddenly had deeper meaning. Needless to say, I passed a sleepless night as I gave in to my swirling emotions. My schedule the next two days kept me from reaching out to Maureen. The fact that I hadn't heard from her only made the public snub even more ominous. On the third day I looked up to find Maureen standing in my doorway. "Hey stranger," she quietly asked. "You got time to go to lunch?" Feeling an odd mixture of relief and fear I grabbed my purse and we headed out.

Have you ever let one small incident get blown entirely out of proportion in your mind? Have you ever found yourself caught in a loop of 'what ifs,' 'suppose this,' and 'could it be' that made rational thought seem impossible? If so, join the worry club. As you've seen, when fear shows up, he usually brings his two sidekicks, worry and anxiety. There is an old adage; to be forewarned is to be forearmed. Therefore, it is vital that we spend some time identifying these two ne'er-do-wells.

What Is Worry?

The Merriam-Webster dictionary gives several definitions that explain the negative emotional impact worry can have in our lives.[13] I particularly like the definition that describes worry as *touching or disturbing something repeatedly*. When you worry, you make a *conscious choice* to mentally touch the thing or situation that causes you distress. You mentally pick it up and turn it over and over, looking at it from all angles. You agitate it until it becomes even more of an issue. Often, something that should be small becomes large because you constantly play with it! In the situation with my friend, Maureen, I had stewed for days over nothing. When I entered the meeting room Maureen had been listening to Karen talk about her husband's infidelity. A kindhearted friend, Maureen was trying to give her full attention to that matter. She attempted to talk to me after the meeting but I had already left. For two days, between teaching and caring for her family Maureen had been counseling and praying with Karen. At the same time, Maureen was worrying about what *she* had done to offend *me*. We had a great laugh and promised to avoid this in the future. For both of us, a small thing became a large thing because of our worry.

For another way to look at this, take an imaginary trip. You've just gotten home after a long day and you're tired. You've had a sense of unease for most of the day and you can't

---

[13] to constrict: **choke, strangle**, to touch or disturb something repeatedly, to afflict with mental distress or agitation, to move, proceed, or progress by unceasing or difficult effort: **struggle,** to feel or experience concern or anxiety: **fret**

quite put your finger on the reason. Not knowing the cause really bothers you. You walk in the front door, drop the mail on the entry table and head into the family room. All you want to do is sit quietly in your favorite chair for a few minutes before the kids come in demanding dinner and energy you're not sure you have. As you enter the family room you notice a small orb laying on the coffee table. You've never seen this thing before and there is something about it that causes a slight constriction in your chest. Rather that walk past it, you pick it up. Although your heart begins to beat a bit faster, you are still fascinated. Your eyes are riveted on the circle you hold in your hands. There appears to be something in the orb that you are not quite seeing, so you turn it around and around, trying to view it from different angles. And every time you turn it around, the orb gets larger and your heart beats faster. Eventually, it becomes heavy and you have difficulty holding it. Yet, you are *convinced* that if you just keep looking at it, if you keep trying to see it from different angles, a new truth will be revealed. You believe you have the power to learn something that will resolve the negative feelings flooding you as you turn that orb around and around. Eventually, the orb grows so large that it begins to press you to the floor. You fall, first to your knees, then, before you know it, you are laying stretch out on your back, the orb pushing you into the carpet. And the thing that you once held is now holding you hostage!

That is the way worries work in your life. You were never intended to turn an issue over and over in your mind. No matter how long you look at it, no matter how

many times you turn it around in your mind, the resolution is not in your abilities. The act of worrying is very much like rocking in a rocking chair. You move and move but you do not go anywhere. You can rock all day long and still not move from one end of the room to the other. Composer, Charles Albert Tindley, captured this sentiment as he responded to a friend about worry, 'My advice to you is put all your troubles in a sack, take 'em to the Lord, and leave 'em there.' [14] The only legitimate reason to grab onto worry is so you can cast it onto Christ who cares enough to want to handle it.[15] Casting your cares is not passive. It has a sense of urgency and energetic action. Casting is purposeful. The fisherman wants the bait in the water where it can attract fish, not tangled up around his feet on the shore. Likewise, you are told to cast all of your cares on God. Keeping your cares close to you increases the odds that you will get tangled up in them. God knows you are not strong enough on your own. However, His strength is made perfect in your weakness. The hymnist wrote 'oh what peace we often forfeit, oh what needless pains we bear, all because we do not carry everything to God in prayer.'[16]

Taking every care and concern to God, with a thankful heart, is the antidote to worry. When a believer commits all of her cares to God in prayer and makes a conscious decision to leave them there, the peace of God comes in. If you are praying and not feeling peace, you may be fretting instead of praying. How do you know the difference? Take an inventory of what you are saying. Listen to how you are saying it. Do

---

[14] Charles A. Tindley, 1916.

[15] 1 Peter 5:7

[16] Joseph Scriven wrote the words to the famous hymn, *What A Friend We Have In Jesus*, in 1855. He wrote these words in the form of a poem to comfort his mother who was seriously ill and living far away from him in Dublin, Ireland.

you feel a sense of release as you share your worry with God or do you find yourself telling God about all of the possible negative outcomes? What is your mind doing when you are praying? Are you able to center on God or do you keep ruminating about the situation? If so, you are not praying. You are fretting!

The world is filled with things about which you could legitimately worry. The economy is uncertain and more people living in poverty. People who have been gainfully employed all of their lives are finding themselves down-sized with fewer options. Paychecks are more difficult to stretch due to soaring utility bills, crazy prices for automotive fuel, high taxes and lack of knowledge about budgeting. Many are part of the sandwich generation. Not only do they still have children to care for but they are also faced with the care of elderly, and oft times, sickly parents. Without a firm faith in God, life would be absolutely hopeless. The world does a great job of convincing us that worry is a natural emotion. And that may be true for those who have not put their hope in the Lord. This must not become the believer's response.

There is no benefit to worry. It always anticipates the worst. Worry wants you convinced that life is fraught with misfortune, trouble, or uncertainty. Worry anticipates a negative future and makes you act as if it is so. Worry pays interest on something that may never happen. The Father of Psychosomatic Medicine, Sir William Osler[17] offered sage instruction on stopping this kind of forward thinking. He recommended that people live in "day-tight compartments." He

---

[17] Sir William Osler (1849-1919), expert in diagnosis of diseases of the heart, lungs and blood, became the first professor of medicine at Johns Hopkins University. Dr. Osler wrote the textbook *The Principles and Practice of Medicine* in 1892 which was considered authoritative for more than 30 years. Known as the father of psychosomatic medicine, Osler combined physiological and psychological treatment of patients and emphasized the importance of the patient's state of mind in achieving a cure.

refused to stew about the future. Rather, he determined to live each day until bedtime. Scripture puts it in different words but the idea is the same; live in "day-tight compartments." *Therefore, I tell you, stop being perpetually uneasy (anxious and worried) about your life, what you shall eat or what you shall drink; or about your body, what you shall put on. Is not life greater [in quality] than food, and the body [far above and more excellent] than clothing? Therefore **do not worry*** (emphasis added) *about tomorrow, for tomorrow will worry about itself. Each day has enough trouble of it own.[18]*

What Is Anxiety?

From the outset I need to acknowledge the important distinction between acute anxiety requiring medical attention and anxiety resulting from a mind that refuses to let God lighten the load. Acute, chronic anxiety can be caused by chemical imbalances or emotional or physical traumas. These require medical attention and are not the subject of this chapter. If you suffer from chronic anxiety, it is important you seek medical assistance. Let God do a healing work through those who are highly trained in this area. Attending to your mental and physical health should never cause shame. In fact, doing so proves your wisdom and maturity.

Anxiety is an exaggerated feeling of worry or tension, even if there is little or no provocation. It is characterized by feelings of uneasiness, apprehension, dread, concern, tension, restlessness and worry. On a practical level, anxiety causes high levels of stress in our lives. According to the American Institute of Stress, 75-90% of all visits to primary care physician's offices are related to stress disorders. "We are at epidemic levels of depression, anxiety, eating disorders,

---

[18] Matthew 6:25,34 Amplified Bible

obesity, type 2 diabetes, heart disease, hypertension, sexual dysfunction, sleep disorders (especially insomnia), osteoporosis, alcoholism, road rage and other forms of violent behavior, PMS, and headaches – and at the root of most of these diseases and ailments we find excessive stress!"[19] Dr. Colbert goes on to say that physicians are treating symptoms instead of the root of these ailments. And while they do, our bodies are not able to shut down the God-given stress response and we are 'literally stewing in our own stress juices.'[20] As the body stores tension over time, a state of chronic anxiety can occur. God didn't intend for us to live like this! David Hazard explains anxiety as an "emotional cocktail made up of one part fear and three parts the sense that something awful and beyond our control is about to happen."[21]

Not only does anxiety have a negative impact on our physical lives; it is a major deterrent to our ability to live spiritually free lives. Luke 8:14 lists anxiety as one of three obstacles that choke and suffocate people so that they are unable to hear and comprehend the word.

> And as for what fell among the thorns, these are [the people] who hear, but as they go on their way they are choked and suffocated with the **anxieties and cares** (emphasis added) and riches and pleasures of life, and their fruit does not ripen (come to maturity and perfection). (AMP)

Being choked with anxiety causes the positive future God intends for you to wither on the vines. Many people never

[19] *Stress Less*, Dr. Don Colbert, Siloam Publishing, 2005, page 6.
[20] Colbert, page 19.
[21] David Hazard, *Overcoming Anxiety, Panic Attacks and Anxiety Disorders: Natural Remedies for Better Living*, Harvest House Publishing, 2003, page 35.

reach their full potential or remain poised on the threshold of greatness because their minds are so filled with anxiety.

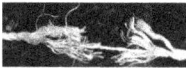

Shredding The Cord:

The enemy wants people to think worry is a natural human emotion given by God. Why is this belief problematic for people who want to be free of worry?

When have you allowed anxious feelings or anxiety to stop you from doing something you believe God called you to do? How will you avoid this in the future?

Donna M. Cox

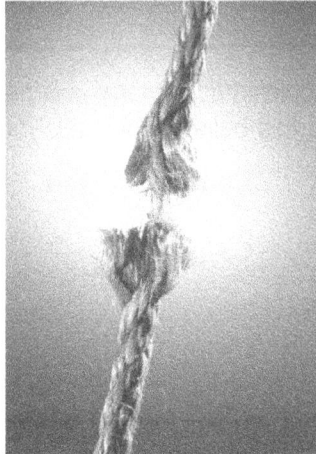

5

The Three-Strand Cord

*"Any concern too small to be turned into a prayer is too small to
be made into a burden." Corrie ten Boom*

There is a principle found in Ecclesiastes 4:9-12[22] that has been
used to teach the power in numbers. Strength is exponentially
multiplied when multiple forces work in tandem. This truth is
one I diligently attempt to teach young couples. They need to
know that standing alone makes them vulnerable and leads to a
weak marriage. Being intimately connected with each other
through deep, personal relationships with God, makes for a
virtually indestructible marriage. When we talk about this
principle as it relates to the presence of Christ in our lives and
in our relationships, the benefits are crystal clear. However,
this scripture teaches an important principle that can be applied
in less positive circumstances. In fact, there is a horrible three-
strand cord we must avoid at all costs! In the last two chapters
we examined fear, anxiety and worry in some detail. In this
chapter we will explore what occurs when we allow them to
combine. Twisted together, these three pack a powerful punch
and can be extraordinarily destructive.

When our daughter was a young teenager, we allowed
her to be at home alone for short periods of time only. On one
of those rare occasions, she was sitting in the family room

---

[22] *Two are better than one, because they have a good return for their work: If one
falls down, his friend can help him up. But pity the man who falls and has no one to
help him up! Also, if two lie down together, they will keep warm. But how can one
keep warm alone? Though one may be overpowered, two can defend themselves. A
cord of three strands is not quickly broken.* Ecclesiastes 4:9-12, NLT

watching television when she heard a sound that startled her. Suddenly afraid, she used the remote to soften the volume on the television so she could listen more carefully. Unaccustomed to being alone in our cavernous home, every creak of the old house seemed even more ominous. She crept to the stairs to peer around the corner, praying she wouldn't find anyone but already convinced someone was in the house. Quietly, she made her way back to the family room and crouched behind the sofa. She began to worry about what would happen when the intruder found her hiding place. Anxiety had her heart beating like the percussion section in the orchestra. She couldn't place a call because the phone was in the other room. Besides, her little voice convinced her, the would-be-murderer would hear her and find her more quickly. Her only weapon was a remote control. She thought she might be able to do a bit of damage with it if she had to... if he didn't have gun or knife. Finally, she couldn't stand it any longer and determined she had to escape. She crept to the window, stealthily opened it, climbed out and made a dash for the neighbor's house. From there she called us. When we got home we found the only open entrance was the window from which she had made her mad dash from the house. Later, we had a good talk about the incident and even a few laughs. Perhaps, you've never climbed out a window because of fear, anxiety and worry but there are probably many who have allowed these three to force them to make similar emotional decisions.

Let's take a look at a similar scenario. Imagine you are at home alone at night. As you begin to drift off to sleep, you hear the normal sounds of a home settling. Your mind processes the sound, convinces your body that all is well and you continue to fall asleep. Fear is defeated. If, however, these same sounds awaken you from a sound sleep, your first response might be fear, a fairly normal response. Though it might take a bit longer you wouldn't remain in fear. Your sluggish mind would sort through the sounds, identify them as ones you had heard many times and you would turn over and go back to sleep. Once again, fear is defeated. Mission accomplished. Fear might cause momentary distress but it wouldn't own the night.

It is not so much *having fear* that is the problem. It is when you allow fear to *have you* that problems occur. When you relinquish your common sense to fear, you wrap yourself with a cord that can potentially imprison you. Let's take the sleeping scenario a bit farther. Suppose you are awakened from a deep sleep by a sound your mind does not immediately identify as normal. As you lay there, with your heart beating rapidly, you recall an article you read earlier in the day about a burglary, clear across town. Worry seizes you. A million questions run through your mind: *What will happen if it is a burglar and he comes in and shoots me? Who is going to feed my fish and dog?* With heart pounding and knees shaking, you quietly get up, creep through the darkened house, jumping at every shadow. At this point, you have two choices. You can recognize that you are being dramatic and everything is fine in your home. You can pray for God's peace, laugh at yourself (even if it is a shaky laugh) and return to sleep, certain that God has everything in control. When you take this option, you break the grip of this two-strand cord, fear and worry. If, on the other hand, even though you find things, as they should be, you return to bed, wide-awake and unable to relax, you allow fear and worry to tighten their grip on you. If you find yourself lying on the bed with the lights on full power recalling every bad thing that has been reported in the news; if your heartbeat continues to accelerate; if your breathing is ragged, your eyes darting from corner to corner; if your hands are clenched, jaw tight and nails digging into your palms, you have just been wrapped in a cord of three strands: fear, worry and anxiety.

The best time to deal with fear is the moment it appears. According to 2 Timothy 1:17, God has not given you the spirit of fear. God has endowed each believer with a spirit of power, of love and of a sound mind! Fear is not from God! Anything you take captive under the power of God can't have power over you. With a bit of personal effort you can win the battle with fear. If, on the other hand, you decide to entertain fear, be prepared for it to invite its partner, worry. Once fear and worry get together, anxiety nearly always shows up. Before you know it, you are wrapped in a three-strand cord and engaged in a serious battle.   Once this happens, you will need heavier artillery to fight. The three-strand cord attacks your mind, soul and body and will eventually suffocate you. Put simpler, it is much easier to defeat fear when it attacks alone.

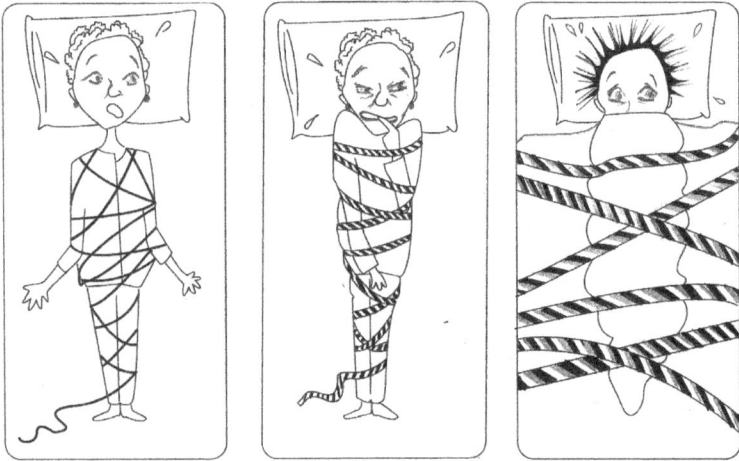

Word pictures help me to understand and remember important concepts so take another mental journey with me. Imagine that you have been bound to a chair. Your captor is merely toying with you so he tied you with a simple, one-ply string. Call this fear. It is absolutely true that you are bound.

But with a bit of work you can break or loosen the string and be free. This is what happens when you deal with fear at the onset. It can't hold you if you put in a bit of effort into stopping it.

Now imagine that your captor tied you to the chair using a braided rope. It is going to take longer to be loosed and there is potential for more damage in the process. We've all seen movies where the hero is tied to a chair by a stout rope. By the time he finishes fighting with the rope his hands and wrists are bloody. His skin is torn and abraded and his body is weakened from loss of blood. This is a picture of what happens to you spiritually when you do battle with the cord of fear, worry and anxiety.

Though it is a difficult war to wage, it is possible to emerge victorious. Scripture teaches that you can do all things through Christ who gives you strength.[23] That includes breaking the power of fear, worry and anxiety. Paula White explains that you can't conquer what you will not confront and you can't confront what you do not identify.[24] This study is fundamentally about identifying the areas of your life where you are strangled by fear, worry and anxiety. After you identify them, confront them head on, trusting God to work as you deliberately, intentionally and *with purpose*, lay them aside. Do not lay them where they can be retrieved. Lay them at the foot of the cross. Charles Tindley expressed it beautifully in his well-known hymn, *"take your burden to the Lord and leave it there. If you trust and never doubt He will surely bring you out. Take your burden to the Lord and leave it there."*

---

[23] Philippians 4:13

[24] Paula White, *Deal With It: You Cannot Conquer What You Will Not Confront*, Thomas Nelson, 2004.

Shredding The Cord:

Identify at least one issue you must confront so you can conquer fear before worry and anxiety kick in?

Think about a time you allowed your thoughts to progress from fear to worry and anxiety instead of stopping the cycle at the initial fear. In retrospect, how could you have responded differently? If this is a situation that may reoccur, create a mantra or statement to remind you to control your responses earlier.

6

The Fork In The Road

*"You block your dream when you allow your fear to grow bigger
than your faith." Mary Manin Morrissey
"Fear tolerated is faith contaminated." Kenneth Copeland*

There is something about the 1994 movie, The Shawshank Redemption[25] that draws me even as it repels. Woven throughout the chronicle of the brutality and corruption of life in Shawshank Prison are profound spiritual truths if one looks. In the movie, viewers witness the power of personal conviction and faith in the face of hardships and tragedy. They also see the devastation that occurs when fear triumphs. Hoodlum inmates purposefully and strategically convinced a heterosexual man he was destined to be a homosexual. They callously and systematically made him believe his value rested in his future role as a plaything for other men. They began by deliberately taunting him and calling him derogatory names. Then they took the plan to the next level. Over time, they raped him repeatedly, all the while painting a mental picture of the intended outcome. In the course of the movie, the transformation of this man, from masculine to feminine, took place. Fear for his life made this man susceptible to the brutality of their attacks. And their attacks were even more insidious because they were not merely directed at his physical body. Their attacks were aimed at his self-concept and they successfully changed the way he saw himself. As a result, this man lived *down* to others' perceptions and purposes for his life.

---

[25] Shawshank Redemption is based on a 1982 Stephen King novel called *Rita Hayworth and Shawshank Redemption.*

49

At the end of this hateful spectrum was the main character, Andy Dufresne (played by Tim Robbins). Like the other man, Andy was beaten and raped by the group calling themselves 'the sisters'. Yet, rather than succumbing to the darkness of fear, rather than allowing his tormentors to shape his identity, Andy maintained a deep faith in his ability to survive and in fact, *thrive* in the face of opposition. Because he never gave in to fear or lost his faith, Andy emerged (escaped) from the system with his sense of self in tact.

Why is it that, subjected to similar humiliation, threats and physical abuse, these men emerged with diametrically opposed images of self? How is it that two men forced to live in the same deplorably hostile and unjust environment had such drastically different outcomes? Sociologists would give several reasons for the different levels of hope each man had for a successful outcome. As a person who has spent years considering the long-term impact of racism and white privilege, I acknowledge the validity of the concerns they would express. While I do not want to minimize these issues I do not attempt to explain the ways. Rather, it is my goal to point to the result of the difference responses each had to the challenges of life behind bars. One man let fear and the opinion of others shape his future. The other let faith be his guiding light. I pause here to issue a critical caveat; I am not advocating Andy's *type* of faith which focused on his own efforts and in the inherent privilege he had as an educated white man. Andy's kind of faith is not the subject of this chapter nor is it a Biblical model. Faith in self is never the same as faith in God. Yet, it is to the underlying principal that I direct your attention; faith always leads to freedom while fear leads to captivity.

The Fork In The Road

You may not be incarcerated or dealing with drama as deep as those in the Shawshank Redemption. However, as long as you are on this journey called life, you will have situations that demand a faith or fear response. I like to think of these as forks in the road. When a problem brings you to a fork in the road, the nature of your response will be fully dependant upon which direction you choose to take. Will you walk on the path of faith or fear? *You* must decide. It is not possible to walk on both paths at the same time because they lead to different destinations. The roads also represent very different experiences. Yet, as impossible as it is, there are many who undertake life's journey attempting to walk in both faith and fear. The result is lunacy. Imagine how foolish it would be to spend a day walking two steps in one direction and then two steps in another. At the end of the day you would be exhausted, frustrated and no closer to a destination than when you started. Despite constant effort, this process will never have a positive outcome. It can never lead to a good solution.

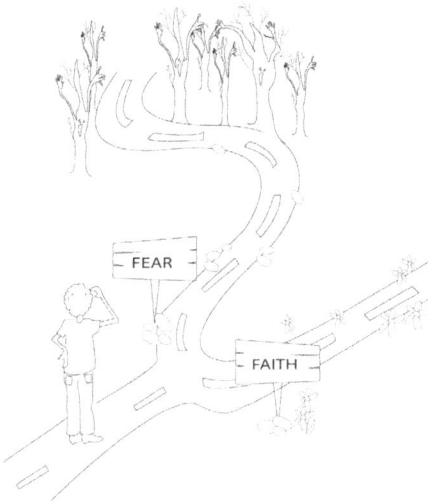

Here is another way to think about it. Try this experiment. Pick up two tennis balls, one in each hand. Now toss them in different directions but follow *both* balls with your eyes. It simply can't be done. Unless you are somehow able to separate the function of your eyes, you will have to choose one ball to follow. That is the way of faith and fear. When you

51

come to that inevitable fork in the road, you must choose which path you will take.

The Path Of Fear

The path of fear is the road most traveled by people who trust in their own abilities. It is filled with people who believe they have to be in control if there is any hope of a positive outcome. People who travel this road have often trusted others and been let down or felt abandoned. So, they succumb to the master illusionist, fear. Choosing the path of fear is a *call to surrender.* If you choose this path you may as well go ahead and wave the white flag and acknowledge defeat. Fear has a *me, myself and I* focus. When you walk in fear, you see everything from a 'me' perspective: *what I believe I can accomplish based on what I know, what I have, who I am and where I live.* An analysis of every problem – no matter how large or small- ends the same way. You size up the threat, compare it to your personal resources and rightly conclude there is a deficit. Like the Israelite scouts in Numbers 13:32-33, fear always makes you see yourself as inadequate. Fear will always conclude that the situation is greater than your ability to meet it.

Instead of admitting the deficit and seeking help, fear sends you into a maze of confusion, false bravado and even more fear. This is the nature of this path. One minute, fear immobilizes you and causes you to lose the ability to think rationally or strategically about your situation. The next minute it makes you think you

52

have found a solution and you end up taking inappropriate action. Before you know it you are helplessly lost and even more afraid. The job of the spirit of fear is to influence your mind, ideas, words, and actions so that you remain lost and isolated from the God who loves you. Fear becomes the tool that Satan uses to get you to a different destination than the one God has planned for your life. Fear will never be satisfied until you are totally ineffective or dead! Satan wants to steal, kill and destroy everything that is good in your life.[26] He steals your peace. Satan kills your spirit and your joy. The enemy destroys, not just your life but that of your family as well.

The Path Of Faith

Fortunately, fear is not the only option when you are faced with a problem. You can choose to take the path of faith. Unlike the inward focus of fear, faith takes a *God-and-me-makes-a-majority* focus. When you are on the path of faith, you can look at the same situation and see very different things. Like Caleb, instead of seeing giants who make you see yourself the size of grasshoppers, you believe you can take possession of the land.[27] Operating in faith doesn't make you unaware of your limitations. In fact, the opposite is true; you *know* you would be woefully under-resourced if you tried to conquer the problem on your own. However, you also know you don't even have to *try*. Faith reminds you that God, who lives and works

---

[26] John 10:10

[27] Numbers 13:30

in you, is greater than any problem you face. Faith says 'I'm not moved by what I feel or see. I've got the victor living in me.' Faith tells you that you have more than enough to be successful.

I've already described the path of fear as a kind of maze. The roads are never-ending. There are obstacles at every turn and fear multiplies. Yet, I don't want to give the impression that a walk on the path of faith is a walk in the park. Quite the contrary, choosing the path of faith is a *call to arms*! Choosing to walk this road means being determined to engage in battle. Ephesians 6:10-18 describes the armor of God you must actively put on if you are to be a successful warrior. Each piece of armor is critical and it would be well worth your time to become intimately acquainted with them. However, I'd like to draw your attention to a particular piece that is very

important in your battle with fear. Verse 16 tells you to "take up the shield of faith with which you can extinguish all the flaming arrows of the evil one." The shield was a symbol for warfare in the ancient world. Ancient Greek soldiers were so connected with these weapons that they were required to come back either carrying their shields if they had been victorious, or being carried on them if they fell in battle. These large shields were covered in leather that could be soaked in water and used to put out flame-tipped arrows. This description was particularly meaningful to 1st Century Christians yet may not be so for modern believers. Faith is always exercised in the context of testing, trials, and problems, including persecution.

If you are going to successfully wage warfare, you must be deeply connected with your shield! If you intend to withstand the arrows of destruction that the enemy will lob at you with deadly accuracy, you must saturate your shield of faith with the living water of God's word. Then you must make a decision to 'take it up.' Taking up the shield requires active engagement and results in faith that is practiced, exercised, used. Every battle you win increases your ability to handle bigger battles. It also clarifies your vision, defines your enemy and reminds you that God is your rear and front guards.

FEAR – Call to Surrender	FAITH – Call to Arms
Me, myself, & I	God and me equal majority 'Not I but Christ'
Magnifies deficits	Has a more-than-enough attitude
Creates stumbling blocks where there might be none	Takes things as they come without adding new weights
Multiplies and breeds new fears	Leads to more and deeper faith
Always winds back upon itself, like a never-ending loop	The path leads to God
Craziness	Stability

The Bridge Of Trust: What To Do When You've Taken The Wrong Path

It is vital that you know and believe all is not lost if you made the wrong decision at the fork in the road. As long as you live, it is possible to change directions. The only way to get from fear to faith is by learning to trust in and rely on God for direction and protection. Leaving fear and moving towards faith requires you to deliberately step off one path and make your way to the other. For many people this transition will feel very uncomfortable. I call this a walk across the bridge of trust.

On one of my trips to Ghana, West Africa our group went to Kakum National Park. In this beautiful, picturesque forest is a series of rope bridges suspended amid the treetops and 120 feet above the Rainforest. For a few cedis[28], visitors experience the wonder of seeing the forest from above. The students in my group decided to take the trek. Because I didn't want to lose face, I decided to take the walk as well. Far from looking sturdy, each bridge looked like little more than flimsy boards wrapped in thick netting. To minimize the swing of the bridge, getting on and off is synchronized so that only one person walks across at a time. Our guide assured us that it was perfectly safe to traverse. He was confident. I was not! My head told me that they wouldn't allow visitors to walk across bridges that might fall apart mid-step. My eyes, however, told me that I would be at least 100 feet in the air, walking on rope tied into knots and wrapped around a 2x15 inch board, sitting on a metal ladder. The netting came to my waist, not above my head, as I would have though necessary. To my way of thinking there was nothing to keep me from tumbling headfirst over the side of this rope bridge! Fear bubbled in my throat and my breathing was shallow – and I had not taken one step onto the first bridge! I asked the guide what would happen if I got halfway and was too afraid to continue. He told me that wouldn't happen. After I pressed him and got the same answer I realized what he meant; once I started across, I had to keep going. There would be no turning back. No one would come to get me.

---

[28] The cedi is the currency used in Ghana.

56

It occurs to me that moving from fear to faith is a bit like my walk across those bridges. Getting up the nerve to start walking is an important first step, one I had to make every time I left the relative safety of the platforms and began to cross another bridge. Fear may be counter-productive but for most people it is also comfortable. You may be tempted to stay put and pray that someone comes to rescue you. However, there is no safety in fear. There is no knight in shining armor that will fly over the hardships and pull you to safety. The platform is only an illusion of safety. Walking across the bridge may be unsettling and at times may tempt you to question the sanity of trying to trust in a support you can't see and can only sometimes feel. As I walked across that bridge, nearly in tears, I could not see the engineering that made it safe to be a sky-walker. From one end to the next, I wondered if I had lost my mind. And, you just might feel the same way about moving away from fear and into faith. Yet, if you just keep moving; if you just keep on trusting; bit-by-bit, step by step you *will* come out on the other side – in faith! God knows every struggle you are going through. God is worthy of your trust and wants you to learn to depend on Him. Just keep moving, just keep going and you will develop a greater ability to trust God, no matter what your eyes see or your ears hear. Trusting God is the only way to abiding in faith.

Scripture is filled with tools you can pull out of your backpack and use at times like this. These tools will give you strength to keep walking, to keep growing in your faith walk. I recommend you go on a search-and-find mission. I have included several of my favorites to get you started.

- Lo, I am with you always, even to the end of the earth (Matt. 28:20)
- I promise never to leave you nor forsake you (Heb. 13:5)
- God is a very present help in the time of trouble (Ps. 46:1)
- God loves me with an everlasting love (Jer. 31:3)
- In my anguish I cried to the LORD, and he answered by setting me free. The LORD is with me; I will not be afraid. What can man do to me? The LORD is with me; he is my helper. I will look in triumph on my enemies. It is better to take refuge in the LORD than to trust in man. It is better to take refuge in the LORD than to trust in princes. (Ps. 118:5-9)
- Even though I walk through the valley of the shadow of death, I will fear no evil, for you are with me; your rod and your staff, they comfort me. (Psalm 23:4 4)

So, we circle back to our starting place. Every person will, at one time or another, come to a point where they must choose a response to the inevitable challenges of life. Which path you choose will be fully dependent upon what you *really believe* about God. When you come to that fork in the road, you must make a decision to believe that God is God. You must decide to believe that God can do what God says God can do. Your situations, the opposing people in your life are not bigger than God. If they are, then you are serving the wrong person.

Choose the path of faith!

Shredding The Cord:

Think of a situation where you have been attempting to walk in faith and fear at the same time. What will you do to move to the path of faith?

You were encouraged to fill your emotional backpack with scriptures. Begin your list below.

Part 3:
Walking The Talk

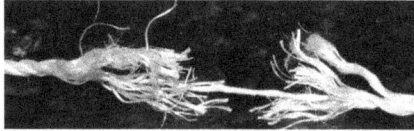

7

Stuck Between The Urgent And The Necessary

"I keep the telephone of my mind open to peace, harmony, health, love and abundance. Then, whenever doubt, anxiety or fear try to call me, they keep getting a busy signal - and soon they'll forget my number."
Edith Armstrong

Thanksgiving has become my favorite holiday. For many years we've hosted a large gathering of family and it's a very special time. We've got the preparation down to a science. I shop; Gerald cleans. Each branch of the family knows what they are expected to contribute to the meal. The menu rarely changes and the men at least, seem to like it this way. We move like a well-oiled machine on Thanksgiving. After eating the great breakfast Gerald cooks, we move about the kitchen attending to the final details of getting the meal ready. Danny peels the potatoes that Gerald will mash later. Noah reminds me how to use the food processor and I slice the yams. Jamie prepares her specialty, deviled eggs. As we've added more children to the mix, the volume has increased. But, there is laughter and lots of fun. The house smells wonderful and mouths water. Overarching it all is a wonderful sense of family, tradition and love. It wasn't always like this. Even though I loved hosting the family, the days leading up to the big event were fraught with tension. Typically, I felt stressed out and worried that things would go well. Underneath it was the unspoken belief that I needed to impress my family to get their approval. So, like a drill sergeant, I issued directives to everyone. I took responsibility for cooking nearly all of the meal. I also did all of the shopping and the planning, down to the smallest details. The list seemed never-ending. *Where would people sleep?*

What food would we have? What stores were having the best sales? What did I do with the children while I shopped? Did I shop after my classes or before? How did I entertain everyone during the holiday so they'd have a great time? By the time Thanksgiving dinner rolled around I was a mess inside. And while the family had fun in another room, I was in the kitchen trying to make sure everything was cooked. I didn't know how to ask for help and I resented that it was not always offered. My perspective on the holiday was skewed and I was out of balance. Some years, giving thanks was the *last* thing on my mind!

At the center of a balanced life is a vibrant relationship with God. Yet, we live in an era that makes meaningful fellowship with God difficult. For women, this can be particularly true. We wear a million hats. In any given day we walk in and out of many different roles. These might include mother, grandmother, wife, sister, daughter, employee, supervisor, minister, pastor, Sunday school teacher, ministry leader, friend, keeper of the family's social calendars, financial aid officer, sanitary engineer, chauffeur, and chief cook and bottle washer. As people of God, it is critical that we learn to balance the many parts of our lives in order to be more effective in the fight for the hearts, minds and souls of our families and communities.

The story of Mary and Martha is a wonderful depiction of the anguish many of us go through on a daily basis. It points to a critical question; will we neglect spending time with the Lord in order to accomplish the never-ending to-do list? Leadership moguls put it this way; *will you allow the urgent to crowd out the necessary*?

Let's take a quick peek inside Mary and Martha's home. One evening Jesus and a bunch of his friends showed up to visit Mary and Martha. Who knows how many dusty men came to their door but we know that the star of the group was

Jesus, the one who had been causing such a stir with his miracles and strange teachings. That alone was enough to cause both Martha and Mary to head into a maelstrom of activities. I heard it said once that entertainment demands certain things of a host: a clean house, good food, well-behaved children, you know the drill. Fellowship on the other hand, says *'Come on in. Sit down. Ignore the children's mess and let's talk."* Clearly Martha was thinking entertainment and not fellowship and for good reason. Convention demanded hospitality. Preparing to feed this group of honored guests, getting their dirty feet cleaned and making sure their household was not dishonored for being poor hosts soon got the best of Martha. Naturally, Mary had begun by assisting her sister but there was something about Jesus that drew her away from the duties of the day and into Jesus' presence. Before she knew it, Mary had defied convention and found herself in a room full of men, sitting at the feet of Jesus. What joy Mary must have found basking in the presence of the Lord. What peace she must have felt! And what made it even more special was Jesus' attitude. He didn't rebuke her for being out of place. He welcomed her! Mary didn't give the work going on around her another thought. And while Mary sat, with her full attention on the Rabbi, absorbing all Jesus taught, Martha was in a flurry of activities. She dashed from kitchen to dining room, snapping her fingers so servants would move more quickly. The harder Martha worked, the more distracted and agitated she became. I can just hear her muttering under her breath! I can feel her anxiety growing as she looked at everything that remained to be done. I know how she felt because this is how I felt many Thanksgiving days! Finally, Martha realized Mary wasn't helping. And frustration mounting, she went in search of her errant sister. Imagine Martha's expression when she saw Mary seated at the foot of Jesus looking like an awestruck teenager! The girl didn't seem to have a care in the world. Her only priority seemed to be *sitting*!

In despair Martha drew a deep breath and demanded of Jesus, 'don't you care that I am doing all of this work and my sister is not helping me? Tell her to help!' I'm sure Martha expected a reply different from what she received. After all, Jesus knew the customs as well as Martha. Mary should *not* have been in the room with the men. She *should* have been helping Martha. That was what was most urgent from Martha's perspective. That was the right thing. Yet, Jesus looked at Martha and saw beyond the immediacy of her aggravation with Mary. He looked deep into her spirit. Jesus saw her anger for what it really was – fear. *"Martha,"* He said, *"you are worried and troubled about many things. But only one thing is needed, and Mary has chosen that good part, which will not be taken away from her."* Instead of getting Jesus' support, Martha was gently rebuked and encouraged to draw near. And this is the irony of the situation. Martha *loved* Jesus. She *wanted* to be with him. At the same time, she had a long list of things that had to be done. Martha was stuck between the urgent and the necessary. She couldn't just cast aside the things expected of her, even if it meant sacrificing personal time with Jesus.

We live in a Martha world, no doubt. Our schedules are so crowded that we sometimes meet ourselves coming and going. And we are busier but not nearly as productive as we used to be. Modern conveniences have put us on call nearly 24-7. The things that were supposed to make our lives simpler have now created situations that make it virtually impossible to relax. We can read and reply to e-mail around the clock. Since transportation is so easily available, we can zip across the country a couple of times in a couple of days. It is not unusual for me to teach until 8:30 pm on Tuesday, catch a 7:30 am flight to go do a presentation, return home Saturday and on Sunday morning attend church, teach Sunday School and meet my choir for rehearsal before a 4:00 concert. No wonder we're tired and agitated. We're getting less sleep and are more stressed. What compounds the issue each one feels is the knowledge that most of what we have to do falls in the category of *good* things. Like Martha, we're stuck between the urgent and the necessary. And being stuck causes us to shift our focus and we begin to ask the wrong questions.

As I read this story, the question Martha's question seemed to leap off the page. Martha, frustrated, tired, stressed out, anxious, and fearful, asked Jesus, *"Don't you care?"* Perhaps because of my own challenges in trying to keep it all together, this question resonated deep in my spirit. I recalled the story of the disciples and Jesus in a boat, crossing to the other side of Galilee[29]. As Jesus lay in the boat fast asleep, a storm gathered and began to toss the boat to and fro. The disciples rushed to Jesus and, just as Martha had done, demanded, *"Don't you care?"* And just as he had rebuked Martha, Jesus took the disciples to task.

In both situations, Martha and the disciples were attending to the business at hand. Martha was trying to take care of her guests. The disciples were manning the boat. Yet, they all seemed to be missing the 'better part' Jesus mentioned to Martha. Two things caused both Martha and the disciples to miss it: they were distracted and they responded out of fear.

Martha was so distracted by busyness that having the Prince of Peace sitting in her living room couldn't fully register in her mind. It certainly didn't register in her spirit. Like Martha, you and I often find ourselves so distracted by all that we *have* to do that we tend to forget that Jesus earnestly craves fellowship with us. And just a moment in the presence of the Lord can give us the energy to make better use of our time. If

---

[29] Mark 4

Martha had begun the visit, even though it was very likely unexpected, by sitting for a few minutes in the parlor with Jesus, her preparations would have gone more smoothly. Instead of the spirit of fear, Martha could have had the oil of joy. And everyone whose lives Martha touched that day would have benefited because of her time with the Lord. Anger is often a mask for fear. Beneath Martha's frustration with Mary was the fear she would be found lacking if everything were not done perfectly. If she had only recognized that the Lord doesn't require perfection, a load would have been lifted from her shoulders. Instead of letting fear make her angry with her sister, Martha could have experienced the refreshing Mary felt.

The disciples were so distracted by the storm they forgot that whatever Jesus spoke came into being. Jesus had already said, *"Let us cross over to the other side."* Implicit in that statement was the assurance they would get there! The fact that Jesus was confident enough to get in the boat and go to sleep should have been a sign to the disciples that they would survive the storm. Instead, they allowed their fear of *what seemed to be* crowd out the reality of *what was.* Yes, there was a storm. That was the reality of what seemed to be. But the reality of *what was* rested in the fact that they were in the boat *with Jesus.* They were in his presence yet they acted as if they were totally on their own. They responded out of fear.

Whenever we keep our eyes focused on the storms in our lives, even when we know Jesus is close by, we will hear ourselves crying out to the Lord, *"Don't you care?"* How many times have you felt this question well up in your spirit? How often are you too busy to spend time with Jesus? How often is your attention so fractured that, even when you are in His presence you end up ignoring him and fretting about other things? Whenever you become distracted by things that *seem to be* most important, you lose the peaceful assurance of *what is.*

You have a Savior who does care. But He needs you to draw near to him.

There is a lot of work to be done. There are children and grandchildren to raise, homes to care for, souls to evangelize, needs to be met. The lists are ever growing. Yet, Jesus is softly rebuking us. Jesus is asking *"Why are you afraid?"* Jesus wants us to see that fear, worry and anxiety are distractions that keep believers from only one thing that's important; time spent in the presence of the living God. Jesus is our example. Throughout His public ministry we find Jesus rarely in a hurry. It didn't matter what people said about Him or to Him. He knew who He was and where He was going. He wasn't held hostage to the demands of others. Sometimes Jesus ignored what some considered a *need* so He could regenerate. Jesus had a vibrant prayer life and modeled it to those under his authority. The message is not new but it is timely. There are always going to be things and people pulling at you. You are confronted by two choices every day. Will you be distracted, worried, overburdened, fearful and angry? Or will you risk being misunderstood in order to make getting into the presence of the Lord your top priority? If you're going to be effective there really is only one choice. You must stay focused on the necessary. You have to allow God to help you manage the urgent and know deep in your spirit that Jesus really does care.

Shredding The Cord:

When have you cried out to the Lord, *Don't You Care?* What was the Lord's response?

How did you get to the point that you could hear His response?

How will you make room for "Mary" on the days "Martha" seems intent on being in control?

8

All That And A Bag of Chips

"Faith is putting all your eggs in God's basket, then counting your
blessings before they hatch." Ramona C. Carroll
"Faith is not trying to believe something regardless of the evidence; faith is
daring something regardless of the consequences" Sherwood Eddy

One Saturday afternoon as I was preparing to go out with a friend I got the phone call. It was the pastor, calling to ask if I planned to be in town the next day. When I said I was, he spoke words that put fear in my heart; 'Will you preach at the 11:00 service tomorrow morning?' I was certain I hadn't heard him correctly so I repeated back what he had just said. Sure enough, he was asking me to preach the next day, at the 11:00 service. Two things about this request brought me up short. First, as a relatively inexperienced preacher and one who *needed* plenty of notice to do *anything*, it didn't seem possible that I could have a sermon ready in just a few short hours. There was no way I could be prepared enough to preach without having time to do the research I thought was necessary. Second, he wanted me to speak at the *11:00 service*! I had never been asked to speak at the *11:00 service*. For just a few minutes my mind convinced me that the *11:00 service* was somehow more important than the 8:00 am service I normally attended. For those few seconds, between the time he asked the question and when I agreed, fear and anxiety held me in their talons. *How was I going to be prepared enough? Was I good enough to handle this assignment?*

I hung up the phone and began pacing the room. *My Lord, did I just agree to preach with less than a day's notice?* I needed to talk to the person that I have always believed could

69

get a word through to the Lord on short notice. I called Dad Cox and explained what had just happened. To my astonishment, Dad began to laugh. I couldn't believe it. Didn't he understand what I had just said? I had to preach before nearly a thousand people with less than a day to prepare. And when was I going to *practice* my manuscript? What was up with Dad? It didn't take long before Dad reminded me that God had already prepared me for this moment. Dad assured me that if God had only given me a few hours to prepare, they were all I would need. Feeling somewhat better yet still anxious, I hung up, sat down and attended to the business of preparing my message. Once I settled myself and started looking through the notes in my prayer journal I realized the truth for myself; God gives us just what we need for the tasks before us. Several weeks earlier I had been journaling and praying about a scripture when the Lord gave me a word. That morning, weeks earlier, I had sat at my desk while the words flowed from God through my pen and into the journal. The sermon I was so anxious about was in my journal, nearly complete!

I wish I could tell you that allowing doubt and fear to seize me in this way was an isolated experience. Unfortunately, I often find myself besieged with thoughts that I am not good enough, old enough, young enough, thin enough, attractive enough, smart enough. My list goes on. And Satan is excited when I fret instead of boldly doing what God wants me to do. Scripture is filled with stories of people who allowed feelings of inadequacy to make them cower. There were many who almost let anxiety and low self-esteem cause them to abort very important missions. From the Old Testament to the New, God has always chosen people, who left to their own devices, would never have walked into their destinies. Let's take a closer look at three of these people.

The Lord called the prophet Jeremiah when he was a boy and Jeremiah responded the way many people might. *'Lord, what makes you think that I can do this? Look God, I'm not old enough! How can you expect me to be a prophet? I'm just a kid. What grown-up is going to listen to a kid they will think is still wet behind the ears? Get back with me in a few years when I'm a little older and wiser and we might be able to work it out.'* Jeremiah wasn't listening to the words the Lord spoke because he was too busy thinking of reasons why he wasn't the right choice. If he had been paying attention he would have heard a key element in his commission. Before Jeremiah's mother and father decided to have a baby, God had already looked into the future of that child and set him apart for a special work. Before his parents even met, the creator of the universe had already selected their baby boy for a special mission. Yet, Jeremiah couldn't see beyond his own sense of inadequacy. Instead of engaging in a debate with Jeremiah, God told him to stop making excuses! Jeremiah's age wasn't a surprise to God. He knew Jeremiah was a boy before the first word was spoken. God had already put his stamp of approval on Jeremiah. But more than that, God had already put his shield of protection around him! And, as a result, Jeremiah could stand and boldly proclaim the word of God!

At the other end of the spectrum is the priest, Zechariah. When he had his encounter, Zechariah was going about his daily work. As was the custom, Zechariah went to the temple to burn a little incense and then he was going to make his way home. Yet, on that particular day and in that sacred space, Zechariah had an appointment with destiny. Standing at the right side of the altar of incense, was an angel of the Lord and the sight nearly frightened Zechariah to death. After telling him to chill out, the Angel told Zechariah that his prayer had been heard. Awestruck, Zechariah couldn't imagine what prayer the angel was talking about. There *was* that prayer about having a baby but he and his wife, Elizabeth had given up all hope that the prayer would ever be answered. Imagine Zechariah's surprise when the angel told him not only was Elizabeth going to have a baby boy, this child would be great in the sight of the Lord.[30] God was going to answer this long-forgotten prayer and God's response was going to be greater than Zechariah had ever imagined! Instead of rejoicing, Zechariah responded just like Jeremiah. He looked at the situation with the limitations of his own experience. *"Do you expect me to believe this? I'm an old man and my wife is an old woman. We ain't having no baby up in here!"*[31] Because of Zechariah's unbelief, he was punished with the loss of his voice until the blessing came to pass.

The final example is also very familiar. Young Mary was minding her own business the day the angel Gabriel stepped out of eternity and into her reality. I can't think of anyone who wouldn't want to be told that he or she is highly favored by God. However this news would totally turn Mary's world upside down. Her life was about to change drastically and permanently. Mary's anxiety was certainly understandable; her confusion and questions were logical. *How can I have a baby? I'm a virgin.* In other words, Mary wanted to know how she was expected to accomplish this task when she didn't have the necessary experience. Gabriel's explanation was the kind of fantastic that makes you drop your jaw and say 'huh?' The spirit of the Lord would overshadow this small-town girl. And as a result of her encounter with the spirit, a special seed would be planted in her womb. Mary, this unmarried, virgin girl was being asked to carry, birth and raise the Son of God!

---

[30] Luke 1:11-17

[31] Paraphrase of Luke 1:18

We know the ends of these stories so you might not really get the full import of what these three people felt when they came face-to-face with the call on their lives. You may have difficulty fully understanding the fear and anxiety they felt during these supernatural encounters. Because you have the benefit of seeing their stories unfold, you might even be a bit critical of their reticence to accept their missions. But, think about it a minute from a more personal vantage point. In each of these examples, God chose someone who couldn't understand how they had gotten selected. Jeremiah believed he was too young. Zechariah thought he was too old and Mary *knew* she didn't have the right qualifications. Yet, each had been *uniquely chosen* and *fully anointed* by God for their appointed work. The limitations that were so obvious to them meant nothing to God. I love the way the Message translation renders 1 Corinthians 1:27-28

> *Take a good look, friends, at who you were when you got called into this life. I don't see many of "the brightest and the best" among you, not many influential, not many from high-society families. Isn't it obvious that God deliberately chose men and women that the culture overlooks and exploits and abuses...*

God chooses ordinary people to do extraordinary things. That includes you. Before the foundation of the world God looked forward through time and space and saw you. God smiled and said *I choose that man, that boy, that girl, that woman.* Ephesians 2:10 teaches that you are God's workmanship. You were created in Christ Jesus to do good works that God prepared, in advance, for you. *Before you were born* God *had already designed* your 'good work' and God is waiting for you to get busy doing it.

What fears are you using as an excuse? Are you trying to convince God to leave you alone because you are not 'white enough, black enough, small enough, rich enough, smart enough, not educated enough, not male enough, female enough?' In the face of God's sovereignty can you really deny that God already knows everything that you consider to be flaws? How arrogant to stand before the one who created you, the one who can count every hair on your head and declare that you are unworthy and unsuitable! The truth is you are all that and a bag of chips! You are fearfully and wonderfully made. You've got everything you need to do and be all that God wants you to do and be. Too many people simply do not believe that. Some believe they are too young or too old to make a difference in this world. Some think they are too poor. Many women have been convinced they are somehow the wrong gender. But if God made you, you're the *right everything.* So shake off the fear, stop arguing with God and stop making excuses. The Bible is filled with young people, old people, folk from the wrong side of the tracks, marginalized folk, people who needed attitude adjustments - folk just like you - whose impact we still feel today, thousands of years later.

Stop comparing yourself negatively to people you think are better educated and more experienced. I've spent most of my life in school and hope everyone will take advantage of the many opportunities available to them. Yet, something happens when you have an encounter with the Holy Spirit that education alone can never replicate. When the spirit overshadows you, when the spirit moves in your life, God will open doors no one can shut and close doors no one can open. And you'll find yourself blessed in ways you could never make happen on your own.

Even as you read this book you may still be convinced that your prayers have fallen on deaf ears. Perhaps you asked God for a special blessing and it's been so long that you no longer dare to hope. But when you ask God for something you have to believe you will receive it. It might not come when you want it but God's timing is always perfect. Don't make the mistake Zechariah made. He gave up on his request and when God declared it would be so, he refused to believe. *Today* might be the day God sends a word that your prayer is being answered. And if you aren't waiting in expectation, if you somehow believe that God's ability to deliver what you want is related to *your* inability, you just might respond in unbelief!

Doubt is one of the greatest tools the enemy can use against you. It is even more insidious because too many times the damning voice comes from within. You look at the situation and out of your own thoughts flow the ideas that shut down the works you've been called, and equipped, to do. Isaiah 55:8-9 says, *"My thoughts are nothing like your thoughts," says the Lord. And my ways are far beyond anything you could imagine. For just as the heavens are higher than the earth, so my ways are higher than your ways and my thoughts higher than your thoughts."* You must bring your thoughts into alignment with God's thoughts. What does God say about you? God says you're all that *and* a bag of chips! You can do all things through Christ who gives you strength. The next time you feel the spirit moving you to take action – go back to school, lead a Bible study, start a business, be kind to the person who's mean to you, feed the homeless, support a ministry, become a stay-at-home Mom, adopt a child, spank the one you've got when he acts crazy – the next time the spirit nudges you to be bold and you feel those old put-downs arise, know, beyond a shadow of a doubt, that these words are not coming from God. The next time the enemy tells you can't do something, roll your neck, throw up your hand and look him in the eye and say *I'm a member of the royal family. I'm the righteousness of God and he loves me with an everlasting love. I'm blessed with every spiritual blessing. I've got a spirit of power, love, and discipline. I've got the power of Christ living and working in me. I'm all that and a bag of chips!!*

Shredding The Cord:

What is the 'thing' that consistently keeps you from moving, with boldness, into your calling? How have you allowed that thing to hold you back? What steps do you need to take to weaken its hold on your thoughts and actions?

With which of the people discussed in this chapter do you most identify? What have you learned from their responses? How can you apply that knowledge to your life in a practical way?

9

Fan The Flame

*"You gain strength, courage, and confidence by every experience in which
you really stop to look fear in the face. You must do the thing which you
think you cannot do." Eleanor Roosevelt*

In Chapter Eight, we discussed the fact that God has already
given you everything you need to be all you were created to be
and to do all you have been called to do. Before you were born,
God already knew what he wanted you to do and what skills
you would need to accomplish the task. While he was deciding
on the shape of your nose and the color of your eyes, he was
shaping your intellect, your passions and planting gifts into
your heart and spirit. Some of you came into the world with
talents that were already clearly formed. Some people, like
Mozart, were able to play the piano and write symphonies by
the age of seven. Some of you were given the gift of
leadership and everyone in your family knew it because you
bossed them around from the time you could talk! Some of
you have the gift of helps and people all over the neighborhood
know to call you when they need anything. For some of you,
your gifts are not quite as easy to identify. Yet, you still need
to be absolutely certain that you *do* have at least one gift. God
does not lie. In Romans 12:6 you are told that, in His grace,
God has given us different gifts for doing certain things well. It
further teaches that these gifts should be used to the best of
your ability. No matter what your talent is, it ultimately boils
down to ministering the gospel. The purpose is the same yet
each will minister in different ways based on the gifts God has
given.

Timothy was a special young man. His spiritual father, Paul, had passed the mantle for the administration of the church at Ephesus to him through a prophetic message and the laying on of hands.[32] Timothy obviously had what he would need to walk out his calling. In his first letter to Timothy, Paul had given clear and specific instructions on the administration of the church. Timothy had been taught well and should have been prepared. Even so, he still needed to be reminded to step up to the plate. In no uncertain terms, Paul told him to start doing what God had gifted him to do. And that is the central message of this chapter.   You must not allow fear, worry, anxiety or any other negative emotion keep you from stepping up to the plate! The gifts God deposited into your life must burn brightly. No one else can do what you were created to do, *in the way* you were created to do it. You have a unique way to serve God and to make a difference in this world. Only you can be you!

An undeveloped talent is an affront to God. It's true that your gift is free. However, it comes with the responsibility – develop it from a tiny spark to a roaring fire. This is what Paul meant when he told Timothy to fan into flame the gift of God. This metaphor is interesting and significant. For several years we lived in a lovely old home that had been a mansion when it was first built. By the time we purchased it, the house was the Money Pit.[33] After a winter trying to heat this un-insulated behemoth and racking up utility bills that could have financed a small third-world country, we knew we needed a plan B. We found a great solution in the form of a wood-burning stove. Yet, the learning curve for successfully building

---

[32] 1Timothy 4:14

[33] Tom Hanks stars with Shelley Long in this 1986 movie by Steven Spielberg. Hanks and Long are a married couple whose efforts to finish construction on their old house are constantly sabotaged by expensive and ridiculous accidents. The unfinished house becomes a metaphor for their troubled relationship.

a fire was steep. Several times we ended up, not with heat, but with a house full of smoke. Sometimes in our zest to create a good fire, we actually smothered the flame. After weeks of working at it, we learned valuable lessons. First, you need seasoned wood to build a good fire. Second, you can't throw just any kind of wood into an indoor stove. To do so means the build-up of creosote inside the chamber, a fire hazard. Third, you have to put kindling in with the right type of wood. After you've got the proper foundation laid, you can strike a match to the kindling. Finally, you need to provide oxygen if you expect the flame to take hold. Making a fire is time intensive. That's why many people would rather go to a wall switch and turn the heat up. Fanning the flame, heating the chamber and continuing to add wood requires diligence and attention if you want a steady fire. The gifts God deposited in your life work much the same way. God puts a gift into you. That's the firewood. God also gives you certain passions. That's the kindling. When you are saved, God gives you a match and tells you to light the fire.

There are multiple reasons many people decide not to fan their flames. However, a close examination of most of them would likely reveal two underlying reasons: shame and fear. It is not accidental that Paul, in verse 8 of the same chapter, warns Timothy about being ashamed, either of the gospel or of Paul. Paul understood intuitively the damage that shame can do. Shame immobilizes a person. Things happen that can color the way you view the world and yourself. Things happen that cut deep into the spirit. Maybe you've been hurt. Perhaps you were used and discarded. Perhaps a parent or spouse abandoned you. Maybe you're a victim of child abuse. These things weigh your spirit down even though you were the victim. But it's not just the things done to you that cause shame. Often, shame results from the actions you've committed. It is possible that your head is hanging low because of your past mistakes and sinful behaviors. Either way, the enemy is thrilled. Shame is an important and regular part of his arsenal and will keep you from fanning your gift into a flame!

The second reason some people don't fan the flame is fear. I have long been convinced that most of people do not fear failure. Frankly, it's easy to fail, especially if you do it often enough. In my own life I've witnessed the ease with which I slide back into wrong attitudes and wrong actions, things that unconsciously make it more difficult to be all God created me to me. Failure requires much less of a person. Succeeding, on the other hand, is much more difficult. Success costs something. It requires you to put aside some emotions that are justifiable. Success requires personal sacrifice. It also demands a level of courage. In his 1994 Inauguration speech, Nelson Mandela quoted the following powerful statement written by Marianne Williamson.

> *Our deepest fear is not that we are inadequate. Our deepest fear is that we are powerful beyond measure. It is our light, not our darkness that frightens us. We ask ourselves, who am I to be brilliant, gorgeous, talented and fabulous." Actually, who are you not to be? You are a child of God. Your playing small doesn't serve the world. There's nothing enlightened about shrinking so that other people won't feel secure around you. We were born to make manifest the Glory of God that is within us. It's not just in some of us. It's in everyone. And as we let our own light shine, we unconsciously give other people permission to do the same. As we are*

> *liberated from our own fear, our presence automatically liberates others[34].*

Fear and shame will make you hesitant to fan the flame but you do not have to give in to them. You have several powerful tools at your immediate disposal. I'll tell you briefly about three.

+ **Tool one: Develop the discipline of reading and studying God's word.** Every moment you spend in the Word fans your flame. Surround yourself with the Word of God. Listen to scriptures in your car. There are excellent (and interesting) audio versions of the Bible. Subscribe to daily devotionals on-line. Meditate on the Word of God daily. As you develop this practice, your flame will grow brighter and brighter.

+ **Tool two: Develop a habit of talking to God about everything in your life.** Tools one and two are complementary. When you read the Word, God talks to you. When you pray, you talk to God. When used together, your fire burns brighter and cleaner because impurities in your thinking, attitudes and actions are burned off!

+ **Tool three: Develop a lifestyle of worship.** Do not restrict worship and praise to Sunday mornings. Recognize the awesome power at your disposal when you focus on the goodness of God. Because God

---

[34] Marianne Williamson, *A Return To Love: Reflections on the Principles of A Course in Miracles,* (Pg. 190-191), Harper Collins, 1992.

inhabits the praises of His people, you literally tap into God's power. If you want God living and moving in your life, learn to praise him. Praise will turn your flame on high!

Satan needs to extinguish your fire *before* it is burning brightly. He needs to take you out while the flame is barely burning. If Satan can convince you that you don't have a gift to use then you won't fan the flame and he can do damage. If he can scare or shame you enough, you will view every wind Satan sends as a tool for your destruction. However, there is another way to look at the winds. Firefighters know they have to extinguish a fire before it becomes fully involved. Once a fire gets to the fully involved stage, there is not much that can be done to stop it. Blowing winds don't threaten a fully involved fire. Instead, the fire *uses* the wind as fuel that causes it to burn brighter and stronger. Blowing winds also carry flaming sparks that create other fires. God created you to be a fully involved fire. When winds of adversity blow, instead of cowering in fear, instead of hanging your head in shame, use them as fuel. TD Jakes writes, "Remember Satan may work feverishly to limit the ministry and reputation of God's vessel, but he can never confine the anointing and the call on your life... negative circumstances reveal Christ, not veil Him."[35] Let every trial make you stronger and more determined to live for Christ. When others see how you survived, they too, will catch a bit of your fire and begin to burn.

---

[35] Insights to Help You Survive Peaks and Valleys: Can You Stand To Be Blessed, Treasure House, PA, 1994

Shredding The Cord:

Identify an area in your life in which the enemy seems to push you. In what way is he trying to extinguish your flame?

How can you flip his actions to fan your flame into a roaring fire?

What practical steps will you take?

Ask a friend to hold you accountable to your plan.

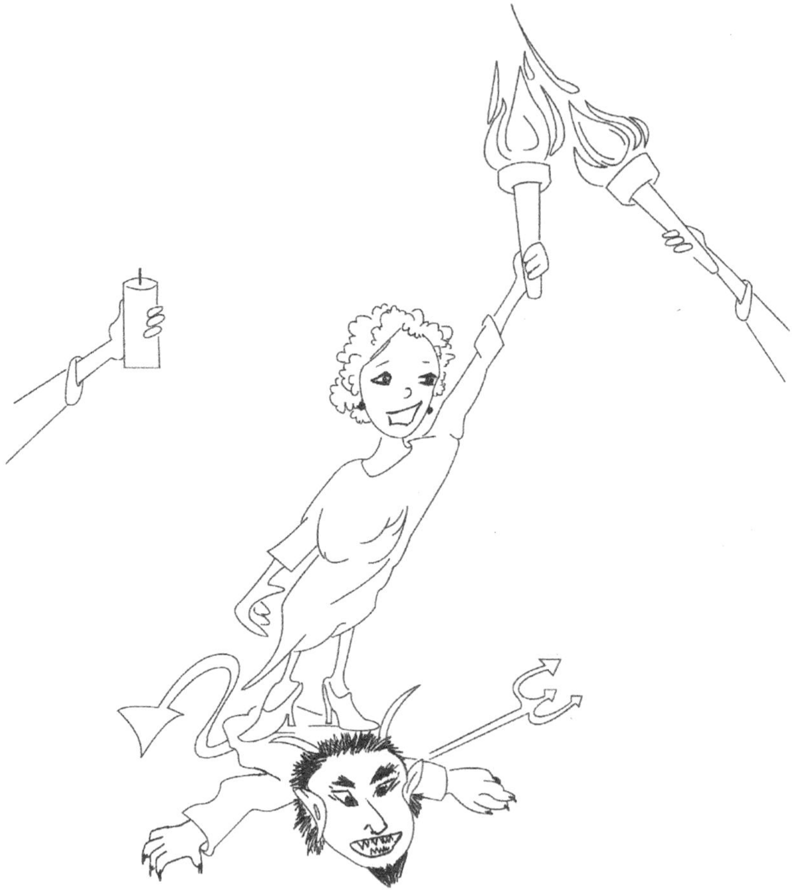

10

Journey To The Well

"Many of us crucify ourselves between two thieves - regret for the past and fear of the future." Fulton Oursler

One of my all-time favorite television shows was the Twilight Zone. You may remember the series. It was created, and often written, by its narrator and host, Rod Serling. Each of the 156 original episodes was a self-contained story that concluded with an unexpected twist. Although advertised as science fiction, the Twilight Zone frequently taught a moral lesson that pertained to everyday life. I liked the distinctive format of the Twilight Zone. Each show began with the trailer that went something like this

> *There is a fifth dimension beyond that which is known to man. It is a dimension as vast as space and as timeless as infinity. It is the middle ground between light and shadow, between science and superstition. And it lies between the pit of man's fears and the summit of his knowledge. This is the dimension of imagination. It is an area which we call – the Twilight Zone.*

And the story would begin. Just when your attention had been captured, Rod Serling would appear on the screen to give the viewer a bit of insider information about the story. Though you rarely saw him again, there was the sense that Rod was around somewhere narrating the story.

In the manner of Rod Serling, I invite you to peek into what, at first glance, may seem like two individuals on a chance meeting. In fact, the two main characters have a divine appointment in the blessing zone. Journey with me, for just a moment, to a well in Sychar, a city in Samaria. When we come upon the well we find Jesus sitting at the edge – weary. He's been traveling by foot from Judea, on his way to Galilee. He's tired and hungry. It's noontime and he's sent the disciples into the city to buy food. And while he waits for the disciples return, he anticipates the *real* reason for this stop in Samaria. Jesus had told the disciples he *needed* to go through Samaria. Certainly, going through Samaria was the most direct route between Judea and Galilee yet most Jews avoided this route and chose to go along the Jordan River. Jesus took this route, not because it was direct but because he had a divine appointment. He knows that today will be a turning point, a day of decision in the life of a very special woman. So, he sits, and he waits for the action to unfold. It doesn't take long before he sees the object of his unexpected stop making her way.

We see a woman approaching the well, carrying her clay water pot. She is hot and dusty. Her face is covered in adherence of her tradition's codes. Her eyes are lowered in accordance with cultural norms. Her shoulders are slumped and, just by the way she is walking, we learn a lot about her. We see the look of the condemned. We see her hopelessness. We see a woman who has spent most of her life on the outside looking in. For some reason today, even though she gave up a long time ago, she finds herself reflecting over her life, her decisions. How did she get to this point? When did she become who she is? She used to have goals. She used to have dreams that one day she would be somebody. When did those dreams die and where had she buried them? Shaking her head at the questions she can't answer – or perhaps does not want to answer – she presses her way to the well to fill her water pot.

As she approaches the well, the woman glances up and she is surprised to see a man sitting there. It's the middle of the day and most people are at home resting or eating the noon meal. 'Darn! What is he doing here,' she thinks to herself. She chose this hour to get water *because* she wanted to be there alone. She didn't *want* to meet anyone else. All of the other women would have already been to the well. They come in the cool of the morning. They come in groups to this gathering place. At the well in the mornings, women connect with other women. At the well, women catch up on village gossip. They discuss their families. They tell the latest stories of their children's antics. They discuss their husband's businesses. They get advice about the garden. Younger mothers ask the older mothers questions about how to discipline their little ones. Teenagers giggle and talk about the young men in the village. The little girls watch their Moms and older sisters and learn how to be women. At the well in the mornings, women are nurtured. In the mornings, women are affirmed by other sisters who understand their plight. They share this chore so collecting water for the family's daily needs isn't such a hardship. Instead, the camaraderie lightens the load.

Yet, our woman goes to the well every day- all by herself. There is never anyone at the well to nurture her. There is no one at the well to share her burden. There is no one to affirm her. There is no mentoring for this woman at the well. Standing there, in the heat of the day, there is no one to give her advice. There is no one who will challenge her to love …. herself. But she has convinced herself she doesn't care. When she goes to the well at noon, there is no one to laugh at her or to talk about her or to put her down. She can avoid the whispers and the jeers. Our woman chooses to go to the well in the heat of the day to avoid the pain she would surely find in the morning. She didn't expect today to be any different. She didn't *want* today to be different. But our lady has a divine appointment and her life is about to be turned upside down!

The woman about to meet Jesus at the well on this day has many strikes against her. First, she is a Samaritan. From the days of the exile, there was hatred between the Jews and the Samaritans. Samaria was the region between Judea and Galilee. When the Northern kingdom was exiled to Assyria, King Sargon repopulated the area with captives from other lands. This led to intermarriages between foreigners and Jews who had not been exiled. As a result, Jews hated the Samaritans, these half-breed Jews. Strike one! Not only was she a Samaritan; she was a *woman*. Women had no clout outside of their homes. Even wives were not acknowledged in the community. Because our woman was a person of questionable morals, she had even less going for her in the gender area. Strike two! Our Samaritan woman was also poor. If she had had money, she could have avoided the well altogether by sending a servant. With the right resources, her entire story would have been very different! And she wouldn't have found herself approaching the well where a strange man sat staring at her intently. Strike three.

Every child knows three strikes means you're out. Yet, this poor Samaritan woman had an even more insidious problem. She had very low self-esteem. Life had taught her she had little worth. She was used by men and disdained by other women. A healthy sense of self could have leveled the playing field somewhat. But self-loathing destroys in a way that ethnicity, gender and social status can't. It destroys the spirit. It kills hope and poisons the future. So, we see her slowly making her way to the well, *in the heat of the day,* shrouded in a sense of hopelessness. Yet, as she makes this ordinary trip to the well she is about to have an extraordinary experience. She has a divine appointment!

Jesus breaks all cultural barriers and speaks to the woman! Not only does he speak, he asks her for water. Naturally, the woman would wonder why he, a Jew *and* a man, was talking to her, a Samaritan woman, and she called him on it. She reminded him of the long, negative history between the Jews and Samaritans. At this point Jesus changes the conversation – from a focus on the physical to the spiritual - and it takes a few minutes for her to catch up. In typical Jesus fashion, he speaks what seems to be a riddle. He tells her that if she had any understanding about the gift of God, she would have been asking *him* for a drink. Confused, she asks how he would be able to help her since he had nothing with which to draw water from the very deep well. Jesus describes the water He offers – water that quenches every thirst; that becomes a fountain springing up into everlasting life. Yet, what the woman *hears* is that she would no longer be thirsty and wouldn't have to journey back to the well. How excited she must have been to think that Jesus offered her rest from the daily grind of her solitary trip to the well. Their conversation takes an even stranger turn when Jesus instructs her to go get her husband – a husband He knows she does not have. Our woman may seem beaten by life but she is not a liar. She readily admits that she's not married. Her openness with Jesus is the first step in her deliverance from pain and a marginalized life. This woman who others condemned, meets the savior and her life is forever changed.

You can learn a lot from the woman at the well. First, Jesus meets you right where you are! Jesus had a divine appointment with the woman at the well and He has a divine appointment with you.   She came to the well with her old water pot. She came with all of her baggage: the pain of living with a man to whom she was not married and the ugliness of having had five husbands. She came with her fears. She brought her shame to the well. What is in your water pot? What stuff causes you to seek water at noon instead of in the cool of the morning? Be honest with Jesus. He knows already and is just waiting for you to acknowledge them so God can move on your behalf. You may be thinking about all the years you were part of the "in crowd." You used to be in the group that laughed and talked about their families. Maybe your house was the place every kid in the neighborhood came to play and eat. Perhaps you used to be the one that others came to for advice. Maybe you spend a great deal of your day remembering how it felt to be at the well in the cool of the morning. And maybe you feel like this woman who had to journey to the well all alone. Maybe you are feeling neglected and angry. Maybe you want to return to the land of the living instead of cowering in the shadows but fear of a painful reception keeps you away. Tell God! Don't keep all of that in your water pot. Bring it to the living water today!

Second, Jesus was not concerned that she belonged to marginalized groups. The fact that she was a Samaritan and a woman didn't bother Jesus. These things didn't disqualify her from service. In fact, the woman left this meeting with Jesus and spread the gospel. As a woman of color I understand her plight. Like her, I belong to two groups who are often at the bottom of the heap. I work and live in a world where my race and gender are often used to negatively define me and keep me operating below my calling. There are days when I forget that I am the righteousness of Christ. There are times I don't act like I am more than a conqueror through Christ! Some days I let people make me believe that I am not worthy of my calling! Yet, as you read in other chapters, this thinking is counterproductive and does not line up with what God says.

Third, the woman felt condemned by her past and her present condition. She had had five husbands and was living with a man to whom she was not married. She kept getting caught up in the same ole stuff. No matter how she tried, she couldn't seem to break the cycle. She was in the same rut, living the same life over and over again. The same stuff kept happening to her. She kept attracting the same kind of men. But Jesus didn't condemn her! In John 3:17, Jesus taught that God didn't send his son into the world to condemn it but that the world, through Christ, might be saved! Whoever believes in Christ is not condemned. People may condemn but we can be assured that God will never condemn those who believe! The woman truthfully acknowledged her sin – that part of her life that she kept hidden in the dark - and Jesus was able to pardon her. Jesus revealed her sin but he didn't revel in it. He didn't explore her sin. He didn't pursue it. He acknowledged it and told her to move on!

What sins are you hiding in the dark? Let the light of Christ reveal and heal every broken place. By exposing your deepest fears and concerns to Christ, you will be made whole. Jesus will not condemn you. God's purpose for sending Jesus was so that you could be saved! As we learned from the experience of the thief on the cross next to Jesus, it is never too late to give yourself to Jesus! You don't have to be baptized. You don't have to jump up, turn around, and clap your hands three times. Just accept the Lord and it's a done deal!

Finally, the woman got it. She understood the message and left her *old water pot at the well!* She left her old self at the well. She left the shame that caused her to avoid others at the well. She left the fear and anxiety that are part and parcel of living outside the will of God. She left the well with a new purpose. She left with a spring in her step, with a sense of hope! She stood straighter and taller. The testimony of her changed life sent others to see for themselves this man who had told her all that she had done.

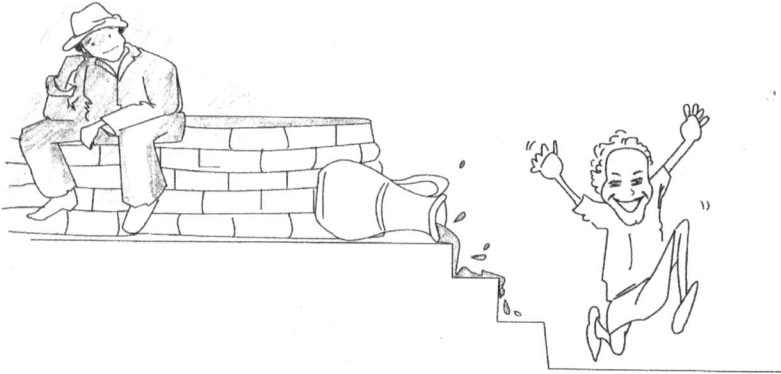

Your journey to the well may be a solitary one. You may go to the well with an old clay pot filled with a lifetime of bad memories, anger, hurt and frustration. Your pot may be crusted over with the shame of having committed grievous sins and fear of condemnation. You may go to the well believing that you are the most unworthy person on earth. But one encounter with Christ, one drink of the living water that only Jesus offers is enough to enable you to leave the pot there and walk away a new person. An encounter with Christ will give you a new walk and with a new talk. You'll get a heart transplant as your heart of stone is replaced with one of flesh. (Ezekiel 36:26) A meeting with Jesus will have you singing the words of the familiar hymn: *Come to the fountain so rich and sweet. Cast thy poor soul at the savior's feet. Plunge in today and be made complete. Glory to his name.*[36]

---

[36] Down At The Cross, words by Elisha Hoffman, music by John H. Stockton

Shredding The Cord:

Are you a member of a marginalized group? If so, how have you been impacted? In what ways have you felt Jesus' love despite what society may say about your group? If you are not, is there an issue in your life that helps you to be empathetic to those who are?

What do you have in your 'water pot' that needs to be left at the well?

Search for other hymns or songs that speak of completeness in Christ? Write out the words and use them as the basis for prayer and praise.

Don't you realize that in a race everyone runs,
but only one person gets the prize?
So run to win!
1 Corinthians 9:24 NLT

11

Take It Off and Put It Down

*"You can't wring your hands and roll up your sleeves
at the same time." Pat Schroeder*
*"People become attached to their burdens sometimes more than the
burdens are attached to them." George Bernard Shaw*

I was sitting in the computer lab in Dublin, Ireland, exchanging emails with my husband who was in Dayton, Ohio. This was several years before everyone had cell phones from which they could surf the Internet. At that time, we had to trek across campus and laboriously log into Trinity College's antiquated email system and pray for a good connection. Most of us discovered we got the best service near midnight so that's when I was having this exchange. Even then, as inconvenient as it was, I was still keenly aware that I live in a fascinating age. With simple strokes of the computer keys and the touch of a button, I could 'talk' to my husband with miles, hours and an ocean separating us. The rapid advances in technology since then make those exchanges pale by comparison. Today, everything moves at warp speed. We cook entire meals in a quarter of the time it took our grandmothers. We can research the world's libraries from the comfort of our homes. We can fly around the world in less than a day.

Yet, for all of the benefits, and there are many, of living in this exciting era, there is a terrible downside. We now expect God to operate like our microwave oven or the Internet. We want instant answers, immediate healing, miracles... right now! We want God to perform so *we* can avoid the work that is ours to do. It has been a frustrating and often painful journey

95

for me to realize that, even though God is perfectly *capable* of removing my weights in a miraculous way, most times God chooses *not* to. Accepting that truth is difficult. I wish I could count the many times I have pleaded with God to simply take away burdens that seemed to press me to the concrete. I've begged God to release me from the weights of fear and anxiety. Yet, because God knows the sweetest victory comes through my own obedience and partnership with God, He chooses not to make things easy for me.

Laying aside any weight or sin that keeps you physically, mentally, emotionally or spiritually bound requires a personal decision to act. When Moses was dispatched to lead the Israelites out of bondage, God didn't beam them out. They had to leave Egypt under their own power. When they got to the Red Sea, they had to step *into* the water for their deliverance. If they had stayed on the shore the story might have ended very differently. In the garden of Gethsemane, Jesus had to lay aside the weight of his frustration with the sleeping, inattentive disciples. He had to lay aside his anxiety over the bitter cup he would drink on Calvary's cross. God told Abraham to leave the weight of his family and to go to a place that would only be revealed *after* Abraham got moving. My point is simple, if you are ever going to be free to successfully run the race God has set before you, every weight – including fear, anxiety and worry – must be purposefully laid aside.

A closer examination of Hebrews 12:1-3 reveals five important steps if you want to successfully move the weights and keep them off. Let's take a closer look at each.

Step one instructs you to lay aside, throw off, or strip off the weight that keeps you from running your best race. My son was on the track team in both high school and college so I have had the opportunity to observe athletes at a variety of experience levels. It only takes one meet before a certain truth becomes crystal clear. No athlete runs a race fully clothed. Before the race begins, it is not uncommon to see the athletes decked out in all kinds of apparel as they stretch or sprint on the sidelines. But when the time nears for the athletes' race, all of the extra clothes are peeled off and abandoned to the sidelines. No matter how blustery the wind, no matter how rainy the day, warm up suits, hats, heavy shoes and other extraneous apparel are removed. These athletes know that added weight makes it difficult for them to run their best.

Too many Christians try to run totally weighed down and it simply can't be done. I recall the time I, as a new faculty member, decided to audit a tennis class. It didn't occur to me that the class would be taught on the outdoor court. We live in Ohio and it gets cold here. The first few weeks of the semester were just fine. The weather was moderate and I found it easy to run up and down the court in my tee shirt and shorts. However, the weather took a quick turn and it was progressively colder each time I went to class. There came a day, late in the semester, when the young graduate assistant teaching the class found me standing on the court - fully clothed in hat, scarf, coat and gloves, acting like I was ready to play. Needless to say my game, which was already pretty poor, was downright awful because I refused to take my extra clothes off.

Hoping to live a successful Christian life while burdened by the weights of fear and anxiety is very much akin to my attempt to play tennis on that cold day. It seems funny but if there were a way to spiritually photograph the heart, mind and spirit I suspect we would find many Christians look just like I did.

Two of the several definitions given in the dictionary are especially helpful in an understanding of weight and why it must be laid aside. Weight is a heavy object used to hold something down. Fear and anxiety keep you anchored to a place God wants you to leave. They attach themselves to you in such an insidious way that some people find it difficult to even get up in the morning. And once they drag themselves out of bed, each step they make throughout the day feels like trudging through a room filled with jell-o. God does not want you weighted down. You were created to live free lives. It is difficult to soar free if you have something that keeps you anchored to the ground.

Weight is also defined as a mental or moral burden or load. Being oppressed in the mind is just as burdensome as walking around each day carrying an hundred pound rock. God didn't intend for you to carry your burdens. Every day you are supposed to transfer the cares of the world from your shoulders to God's. Psalm 55:22 tells you to cast your burden on the Lord and He will sustain you. When you attempt to carry your burdens on your own you set yourselves up for failure. You have enough energy supplied for your daily trials. You can't expect to successfully maneuver *today* if you are burdened by memories yesterday and concerns for tomorrow. Yesterday is gone. Nothing you do will ever change what happened yesterday. The failures of yesterday have had their moment. Continuing to fret over them today serves only to use the precious allotment of grace and energy, things God designed to support you through today. This is one of the reasons some people are physically, mentally and emotionally exhausted every day. They are trying to go through their present oppressed by all of yesterday's problems.

And as if that were not enough, they even borrow a few imagined problems of tomorrow. Imagine, for a moment, this scenario. Early one morning, you grab the clothes you decided the night before to wear to work and begin to dress. While you are dressing, an internal voice reminds you of an important meeting you will lead the next day. Before you think about it, you start selecting the power suit you believe will help you to feel more confident. The voice continues to remind you of those who have been challenging your leadership and you feel anxiety start to increase. You stop by the mirror to get one last look before you leave your bedroom and you are totally amazed by what you see. There you stand, fully clothed in the outfit for today *as well as* the ones you selected for tomorrow! Before you laugh too hard at the absurdity of this scenario, think about how your emotions are clothed. Tomorrow is not promised. Borrowing problems from tomorrow is just as silly as getting up today and putting on all of the clothes you intend to wear tomorrow. Today's trials are sufficient for today. Every day God gives you just enough grace to get through this *one day*. You were not designed to carry the weight of yesterday and tomorrow with you in the present.

Step Two tells you to run, with endurance, the race that has been set before you. The ability to run with endurance begins in the starters block. Each athlete has two goals: getting out of the starting block and finishing the race. Too many people allow fear and anxiety to keep them in the starting block. Or they start the race and then half way around, when they see other runners advancing, they walk to the sideline and, like a pouty child, sit down. And there they sit, stewing in anxiety over what might have been! The best athletes decide, *before the starting gun,* that they will complete the race. Even if they run a bad race, or have an accident, if it is physically possible for them to cross the finish line, they do so. One of my favorite movies is *Cool Runnings[37].* The ragtag team of sledders from Jamaica wages a valiant effort to be able to compete in the winter games. Just when it looks as if they have a shot at a positive showing, they have major sled problems. But what makes the story so very encouraging is how they handle this disappointing setback. With heads held high, these brothers pick themselves up, shoulder their sled and walk across the finish line while the onlookers gradually begin to applaud. God wants you to have this same kind of tenacity when it comes to your life. 1 Corinthians 9:24 asks and answers an important question. *"Don't you realize that in a race everyone runs, but only one person gets the prize? So run to win!"* It goes on to state in verses 25-27 *"All athletes are disciplined in their training. They do it to win a prize that will fade away, but we do it for an eternal prize. So I run with purpose in every step. I am not just shadowboxing. I discipline my body like an athlete, training it to do what it should. Otherwise, I fear that after preaching to others I myself might be disqualified."* (NIV)

Just as it makes little sense to stay in the starting block, you can't run someone else's race. The word says that you are to run the race that is set *before you.* You have to run your own race. You need all of your strength, all of your wits just to run the race that God has set *before you.* This is the only race God gives you the grace and strength to finish. Fear takes the focus off of your own race and shifts it to someone else's. You worry about your children and waste your store of energy trying to run for them. Married women often choose to run their husbands' races as leaders of the home and become

---

[37] Directed by Jon Turteltaub in 1993

burdened by anxieties that were never supposed to be theirs to carry. We do this on our jobs, in our homes, and even in our churches. And we wonder why life seems so hard. As a mother of two adult children, I often find myself trying to run their race. Because I have the benefit of experience, I can often see roadblocks they don't see. Yet, instead of praying, I find myself fretting. Or I give advice they may not welcome and worry over their choices. That's trying to run a race that is not my own.

Step three tells you to fix our eyes on Jesus, the author and finisher of your faith. There is no way to successfully run a race while looking behind you and worrying about what you have already passed or fretting over what may be coming. The Christian race requires the same kind of discipline. We have already seen how foolhardy it is to continue looking behind and worrying about the past. Likewise, you can't run a successful race if you are busy looking left or right. Turning your head from side to side wastes precious energy. What are some of the ways you turn from side to side? You do that when you allow your mind to be flooded with repetitive, negative "what if" statements. *What if my position is cut in the next round of layoffs? What if my colleagues talk about me? What if my daughter gets pregnant? What if I get breast cancer? What if I don't get the job?* What if, what if, what if? 'What ifs' take your attention off of Jesus and weaken your confidence.

Where you direct your eyes is extraordinarily important. The things you look at the longest, whether negative or positive, are the things that become magnified in your mind. I love the apostle Peter because I see so much of myself in him. When confronted with Jesus walking on water, Peter wanted to do the same. He made the right moves; he laid aside his fear; he got out of the boat; he fixed his eyes on Jesus; Peter walked on water! When he stopped looking straight ahead he became

101

caught up in the realization that people do not walk on water! Fear robbed Peter of the ability to do something extraordinary. When you start to sink in things you used to walk on, you need to take a quick survey of where your eyes are focused. Ask yourself what you are looking at that is feeding the anxiety. Shifting your eyes away from that thing and focusing on Jesus is a certain life preserver.

Step four is a reminder to consider the one who endured hostility lest you become weary and discouraged. The word *consider* is crucial to really understanding this step. To consider something means to study, contemplate, weigh, to think about in order to arrive at a suitable conclusion, opinion or decision. To consider means purposeful concentration and paying attention to details. A deep consideration of an item, an event or an idea often implies balancing conflicting claims or evidence in order to reach the best conclusion. Inherent in this step is a very important principle. To successfully run your race, you must study the techniques of others. From them you can learn how to stay encouraged, even in the midst of suffering, disappointments, trials and tribulations of all kinds.

Athletes routinely watch films of past races. They study the techniques of the winners. They also critically review their own performance. The purpose of this endeavor is not for team members to beat themselves up about what they did wrong. Nor is the purpose to worry and fret over the talents of the competition. This process forces team members to analyze *why* the winner won and to learn from them. Likewise, you need to seriously consider people who are winning in the race of life. There are wonderful stories between the pages of the bible that teach about faith that transforms the ordinary into the extraordinary. They point you to a God who never changes, a God that can and will do for us what was done for the saints of old. Hebrews 11 is filled with inspiring examples, heroes of the past that demonstrate the power of personal faith and God's unswerving desire to meet that faith with awesome power. The full account of the heroes of the faith extolled in Hebrews 11 as well as countless others are recorded in the word of God so that you can grow in your own faith walks. In each case, it was necessary for the person to cast off a specific weight or a particular sin in order to move forward in the power and might of God. And as you consider their examples you can apply proven techniques to our own situations and live more victoriously.

Step five is an encouragement to seek joy instead of happiness. Jesus' attitude provides a powerful example. The scripture teaches that Christ went to the cross for the *joy* that was set before Him.[38] In a world that seems to put tremendous stock in the pursuit of happiness, you have to deliberately choose the joy that comes from knowing that you are being obedient and doing what God has called you to do. It is your task to be motivated by joy instead of seeking the fleeting emotion of happiness. Joy is a deeper emotion that comes from internal wellbeing, a sense that your life has meaning and purpose *regardless of temporary situations*. On the other hand, happiness is derived from feelings associated largely with external factors. Feelings of happiness are most often dependent upon how others treat you or what is going on in your life at any given moment. It is possible to be temporarily happy and have no lasting joy. At the same time, it is possible to possess deep joy and still have feelings of unhappiness. You can be certain Jesus was not *happy* about the prospect of being crucified. In fact, he pleaded with God to remove the threat of the cross if it were possible. Ultimately, Jesus decided to ignore the unhappiness He felt to focus on being in God's will. Like Jesus, you must be motivated by joy instead of happiness.

---

[38] Hebrews 12:2

A story is told about a Cherokee chief's conversation with his grandson. The boy had broken a tribal taboo and his grandpa wanted to help him understand what made him do it. "It is as if we had two wolves inside of us," said the chief. "One wolf is very good. The other one is very bad. Both of the wolves demand our obedience." "Which one wins?" asked the little boy. "The one that we feed" replied the wise old man.[39]

Releasing fear and anxiety is a choice. Every day you must choose to feed your faith and not your fears. You choose, deliberately, to release the weights of fear, anxiety, and worry. You purposefully lay them aside. You do not expect God to do work you have are empowered to do. You run with deliberate intent. You fix your eyes on Jesus and keep them there no matter what the situation looks like. You consider the successes of others and learn from them and you look for the joy that is evident in every situation when you are in the will of God.

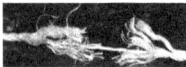

Shredding The Cord:

A popular phrase today is 'stay in your lane.' When have you found yourself in someone else's 'lane?' Whose race have you tried to run that really is not yours to run? Try to identify the emotions that propelled you to make that move. How can you avoid this in the future?

---

[39] Author unknown

If you could take a spiritual photograph of your mind and heart, what extra weights would you see?

Visualize peeling off every care and placing it at the foot of the cross. Allow yourself to experience easier breaths as you are released. Do **not** pick them back up.

Do a praise dance every time you are tempted – the sillier, the more energetic, the better. Thank God for caring!

This charge I commit to you,
son Timothy, according to the prophecies
previously made concerning you,
that by them you may
wage the good warfare
1 Timothy 1:18 NKJV

12

Strategies for Successful Warfare

"Worry, doubt, fear and despair are the enemies which slowly bring us down to the ground and turn us to dust before we die."
Attributed to Douglas MacArthur
"If you see ten troubles coming down the road, you can be sure that nine will run into the ditch before they reach you." Calvin Coolidge

It seems as if nearly every waking hour of the seven years I served as Department Chair I was writing a strategic plan of one kind or another. First, we were getting reaccredited. That was a huge undertaking and took over two years of my life. Then there were a zillion other reasons why we needed to think strategically about something. When I started, I didn't have a clue about how to write a strategic plan. So I began to read and talk to people I knew were great strategic thinkers. I learned that if a strategic plan is to work it must be a living, breathing document that governs the actions of the organization. I also learned that every strategy had to have specific action steps and you should be able to assess the action steps. In other words, at a specific time in the future we should be able to gauge just how well the action steps were carried out and if the strategy was successful. Strategic plans and action steps should also have ownership! If a task is defined as important, there has to be someone responsible for making sure it takes place. At the end of the day, I realized that a strategic plan was no good if you put it on a shelf somewhere and let it gather dust.

And while I was busy writing plans for the department the Lord helped me draw some personal parallels. Each individual must learn to think strategically about his or her life. If she doesn't, she will end up wasting time on activities and

107

endeavors that lead nowhere fast. We all know people who seem to be wandering, trying first one thing then another. And before they realize it, they are 30 and they've wasted the 20s. Before too long they realize they are 60 and wonder where their youth went. Being able to think and act strategically are skills each person needs to hone. But these skills are not simply for determining career and family paths. Each person in the army of the Lord, every man, woman, boy or girl who decided to follow Jesus Christ, must recognize they are engaged in a critical battle. And if the battle is to going to be fought successfully, if the battle is going to be won with minimal losses, the soldiers need to have a strategy for waging successful warfare.

This is the story about Jehoshaphat, the king of Judah. For the first few years of his reign Jehoshaphat enjoyed much prosperity and a peaceful kingdom. The blessings of God seemed to be all over his life and everything he touched prospered. Then he did a really stupid thing. He entered into an alliance with Ahab, the king of Israel. This brought disgrace and near disaster to his kingdom. Jehoshaphat escaped the battle in which Ahab died but his reputation didn't escape unscathed. He had a long road to recover his former relationship with God. But he did it. He was determined to turn his kingdom back to God. He deepened his personal relationship with God and began to clear the kingdom of all forms of idolatry. He appointed judges and other leaders to rule over the people. Jehoshaphat had a new attitude! He had a different kind of pep in his step. He was on fire for God and determined to stay that way.

Then, from out of nowhere came the report that a great multitude was marching against his kingdom! Maybe you can identify with Jehoshaphat. Perhaps you used to live carelessly. Maybe you made bad decisions and were on a path to destruction. Then you gave your life to Christ. With God's

108

help you started to clean up your act. You made restitution to the people you hurt and your life was 180 degrees from the way you used to live. It seemed as if things were going pretty good. Your finances seemed to be in order. Your children were acting right. You had lots of reasons to laugh and smile. I hate to be the bearer of bad news but this is the truth. No one is immune to a surprise attack. Just when you think you're on level ground; just when it looks like life can't get any better, a simple phone call can make you feel like the bottom is about to drop out.

This is how Jehoshaphat must have felt. The armies of the Moabites, Ammonites, and even some of the Menunites were declaring war on Jehoshaphat and his people! When Jehoshaphat heard the news, he was alarmed! In reality, he had very good reason to be concerned. He knew the reputation of these people because they had a long history together. The bad blood between them went way back. Jehoshaphat was understandably just a bit scared! His reaction should encourage you. Don't beat yourself up when an impending assault causes you to feel alarmed or afraid. It would be crazy to shrug it off. Only foolish bravado would make you say "it ain't a thang. I'm not worried." Jehoshaphat was alarmed but he knew exactly what he needed to do. If you're going to be successful in warfare of any kind - personal attacks, unexpected or lingering illness, empty bank accounts with a mound of unpaid bills, or even loneliness - if you are going to wage a successful war, you've got to do what Jehoshaphat did! He was determined to seek the Lord.

Strategy Number 1: *Seek God's power, not your own.*

You may as well admit there are things that can cause your breath to hitch and your steps to falter. Fear is not the problem. It's what you do with your fear that messes things up.

Soldiers who have been trained for the battle acknowledge their fear and immediately take it the throne of God! When he heard the bad news, Jehoshaphat didn't start plotting his own defense. He didn't hide in a corner of the kingdom where he thought he wouldn't be found. He didn't pack his people up and leave the kingdom on a run. Jehoshaphat immediately sprung into action! He proclaimed a fast in Judah and gathered people from all over to have a talk with the Lord. (v. 13) Like Jehoshaphat, sometimes you need to gather all of your family or all of your friends together to seek the Lord! Most of us do call people when we're alarmed but it's typically not to seek God. We call them to rehearse and rehearse what's going on. *'Chile, don't you know that Sandy has gotten half of the people in the shop to tell the boss lies on me. Last year when she was coming to work late everyday, I could have reported her butt to the boss but I didn't do it. Now she goin' round messing with me. Well I ain't gonna take it.'* You know the story. Sure, you sprung into immediate action but not one thing you did was positive or productive.

Jehoshaphat understood the words of the psalmist who said, *"Though an host shall encamp against me, my heart will not fear; though war should rise against me, in this will I be confident." Ps. 27:3* He knew that it wasn't his own power that he was depending on! Jehoshaphat stood in the presence of the Lord and prayed. *"O LORD, God of our ancestors, you alone are the God who is in heaven. You are ruler of all the kingdoms of the earth. You are powerful and mighty; no one can stand against you! O our God, did you not drive out those who lived in this land when your people arrived? And did you not give this land forever to the descendants of your friend Abraham? Your people settled here and built this Temple for you. They said, 'whenever we are faced with any calamity such as war, disease, or famine, we can come to stand in your presence*

110

before this Temple where your name is honored. We can cry out to you to save us, and you will hear us and rescue us.'

Why did Jehoshaphat begin his prayer with these reminders to God? Was he worried that God had amnesia? Did he think God's memory was selective like ours can be? Did he expect God to have changed his mind about his promises? No! These reminders weren't for God. They were for Jehoshaphat and the people of Judah!

Strategy Number 2: If you're going to be successful in warfare, you've got to remember your history with God and your legacy *in* God!

Jehoshaphat was clear about who was. He knew he had a blood covenant with God and he expected God to honor it. Jehoshaphat was also confident because he recalled the many ways God had delivered him in the past. Even though he was alarmed, Jehoshaphat knew he was not alone. Because he was from the seed of Abraham he knew God was honor-bound to protect him, his people and their land. Likewise, if you're a child of God you have a blood covenant through Christ. You have a birthright of provision and protection. The Bible is filled with God's promises for those who put their trust in Him. Yet, you've got to know what they are if you expect to take advantage of them. If someone gave you a million dollars but put it in a bank and didn't tell you the name or account number, it would be virtually useless. You might as well be totally broke. Yet, if that same million dollars were put in a bank and you were given all of the necessary information you'd be sitting pretty. You could make a withdrawal anytime you needed to. In the same way, you are an heir to the promises of God. The information isn't hidden but you do have to know how to access it. You could save yourself a lot of anxiety if you just took time to remember all the ways God has provided in the past. You don't need to go back fifty years. What has God done for you lately? Have you seen the hand of God deliver you from a situation that caused you to say, as Jehoshaphat said, *I don't know what to do but I am looking for you to help!* Remember and know that if God did it once, he can certainly do it again!

Imagine how Jehoshaphat might have been feeling as he cried out to the Lord. A generation earlier, when Israel had the opportunity to destroy the Ammonites and Moabites, God wouldn't allow them to do so. In his prayer Jehoshaphat reminded God about this. I can just hear Jehoshaphat saying, 'now God, when my ancestors could have destroyed these evil folk, you wouldn't let them do it. Instead of letting them kick some serious butt, you led them the *long way around.* Now, after all this time, here come their relatives ready to attack and kick us out of the land you've given to us! Didn't you say that this is our land *forever*? That was the promise you made to my great granddaddy, Abraham. Doesn't that promise extend to me? Are you going to let this happen, God?'

I know how Jehoshaphat might have been feeling because I've often felt the same way. Many times the perfect opportunity to strike back at people who've tried to harm you presents itself like an unholy gift. It seems like you are in the perfect position to take them out. But God, by his gentle spirit, touches you and says 'no! Leave them alone! Go the long way around.' And even though you might not want to, even though it doesn't make any sense, you are obedient to the Lord. You leave them alone. You think that means that you won't have to deal with this issue again. Then these *same people* – the ones God wouldn't let you mess with- turn around and pay you back by launching a surprise attack. It doesn't seem to make much sense. It didn't make sense to Jehoshaphat so he reminded God of the injustice of the attack.

112

And while Jehoshaphat was standing there praying his heart and worries out to the Lord, he received his answer. That's just like God. Many times, while you're trying to figure out the problem, God has *already* dispatched his messenger. While you're telling God you don't know which way to go, He's already sent someone to show you the door. Even as Jehoshaphat was praying, the Spirit of the Lord came upon Jahaziel who spoke the words of God: *Don't be afraid! Don't be discouraged by this mighty army, for the battle is not yours, but God's. Tomorrow, march out against them.*

Strategy Number 3: The war is not about you so the battle is not yours!

This is an important truth. The attack on your family, on your finances, on your health, on your marriage, whatever the attack, it is not about you. You're just a pawn in an eternal battle between Satan and God. And if you are to wage successful warfare, you must realize this. The war is not about you so the battle is not yours. Scripture teaches that you don't wrestle against flesh and blood but against the principalities, against powers, against the rulers of the darkness of this age. (Ephesians 6:12) Stop trying to fight a spiritual battle with the weapons of this world. They simply will not work. God is the master strategist and if you would take your burdens to the Lord rather than trying to shoulder them yourself, you'd be so much better off. The hymnist writes, *oh what peace we often forfeit. Oh what needless pain we bear. All because we don't carry everything to God in prayer!*[40]

The battle isn't yours but you might have to participate. God could have turned the Moabites and Ammonites back.

---

[40] *What A Friend We Have In Jesus*, written by Joseph M. Scriven (1820-1886) and Charles C. Converse (1832-1918)

They could have been ambushed on their way by one of their enemies. God could have made it so that Judah didn't have to participate in the battle at all. But God didn't do that. And there is something very important to learn in this. Sometimes God protects you from enemies you don't even see. If you could part the veil you'd see the many times God kept you from being destroyed without your awareness. God is able to do that. But for many of your battles, God will require you to be an active participant in your victory. And the part that you have to play is very important.

Every strategic plan has to have action steps. The word the Lord spoke to the people of Judah is a fundamental step: *Don't be discouraged. Don't be afraid.* The word does not say, try not to fear or try not to be discouraged. These are emphatic statements. You have the power of choice. You can choose to look at that powerful enemy and become despondent and afraid or you can choose to believe that the battle is the Lord's and therefore victory is assured. It is your job to control how you think and feel about the situation. I know this is hard - especially for those of you who wear your emotions on your sleeves. Stop being discouraged. Stop being afraid. Stop looking at the enemy and start looking to God! God has not given you the spirit of fear! That's your first action step. And the second step is summed up in the last strategy.

Strategy Number 4: Praise your way into a new reality!
This was mentioned in the last chapter but it bears repeating. You must understand the awesome power you have at your disposal in the form of worship and praise. God loves praise and God deserves your worship. Though they work together, they are not the same. When people do good things, you praise them. You tell them what a good job they did. You clap your hands when the choir sings beautifully. You stand and yell when your favorite team scores a point. That's what

praise is. When you praise God you thank him for what he has done! You thank Him for the new house, the promotion, and the good test results. Worship goes much deeper. Worship means to ascribe worth-ship to God. Worship recognizes God for who God is. Praise is thanking God for what God has done for you. Worship says if God doesn't do another thing, you are grateful just because of who God is!! When you worship God you activate your faith by laying claim to the promises inherent in God's very character!

The people of Judah understood the power of making a joyful noise before the Lord and you can find examples throughout history of this in action. During the Civil Rights movement people used song to claim ownership of the air and to make bold statements to their persecutors. If you have children, you've also seen this same principle at work. Just try to get a two-year old to do something they don't want to do! How many times have you seen a mother tell a toddler to do something only to hear the child break out into a song? And the louder the mother talks the louder the kid sings. It really doesn't matter what you do if the child is stubborn enough. When she is asserting her independence in a loud voice, with her face to the floor, you might as well give up!

You have got to be like that two year old in facing down your fears! Be bold. Lift your voice to the Lord and shout for joy! Praise your way into a new reality. Worship your way into a new understanding. Even if it seems like an entire army is marching against you, begin to worship and God will change your reality!

Praising and worshipping God may not stop the enemy's assault. Even while you are worshipping, they may be steadily approaching. That's your present reality. But worshipping God can *change your perspective*. And once your perspective is changed, you begin to rest in God's assurances that He's with you even though you might be walking through the valley of the shadow of death![41] Jehoshaphat and the people of Judah *knew* the enemy was approaching. This was a fact. And standing in the temple didn't stop their approach. At the same time, they heard God say that they wouldn't have to fight! There was a moment when their belief in God came face-to-face with their present reality! They had to choose which reality they would believe. Don't miss this. They heard the word of the Lord say they wouldn't have to fight *even though* they saw the enemy advancing. In that moment they had to choose what they would believe. So, they fell on their face before the Lord in worship! They had a big battle to win and their praise and worship had to be bigger! On the day of the battle they began their march to the battlefield with songs of thanksgiving! That's what you've got to do. Raise your voice in worship and praise and declare your present reality to be a lie! Look at your empty wallet and call it a liar. Look at your wayward child and declare her positive future. Look at cancer and say *by His stripes I'm healed*! Don't confuse fact with truth!

This is the strategic plan for successful warfare. The strategy works if you work it!

1. **Seek the Lord's power not your own.** You will never be able to win in your own might! Not by might, not by power but by my spirit says the Lord!
2. **Remember your history with God and your legacy *in* God!** Learn the promises and stand on them.
3. **Remember that the war is not about you so the battle is not yours!** Sing like the old saints, '*if I hold my peace, let the Lord fight my battle, victory, victory shall be mine.*'

---

[41] Psalm 23:4

4. **Worship and praise your way into a new reality.** It is virtually impossible to really praise the Lord AND be afraid at the same time. I'm not talking about a passive praise but one that comes from deep within your spirit because you *know* that God has been good to you. If you don't believe me, try it the next time your heart is broken. Strike up a song of praise to the Lord and see how things begin to change for you. Tell Satan his party is cancelled and you are throwing a freedom festival. You are no longer afraid!

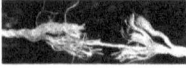

Shredding The Cord:

Think about a time in your life when what was **fact** did not line up with the **truth** of God's word. Which did you choose to believe? What was the result?

What situation is currently causing you the most fear? Choose your favorite praise song, turn the volume on high and worship until you are able to step back from the problem and hear whether God wants you to stand still or participate in the battle.

118

Rev. Dr. Donna Cox

Rev. Dr. Donna Cox is a graduate of Washington University in St. Louis where she received both the Ph.D. and M.M. degrees in Performance Practices: Choral Conducting and the University of Dayton where she received the M.A. in Theological Studies. In addition to serving as Chair of the Department of Music for seven years, Dr. Cox directs the Ebony Heritage Singers, the University gospel choir. A much-sought lecturer and choral adjudicator, she has presented educational sessions at state, national and international conferences throughout the United States and in various parts of the world.

Dr. Cox has ministered, performed, studied and taught in various parts of the world including Dublin, Ireland where she and a small group of singers opened for the 1998 *Tour de France*. Dr Cox has performed recitals of African American Arts Songs and Spirituals in Ireland and London. She has traveled several times to Ghana, West Africa to conduct choral and vocal workshops and master-classes and has been featured in recital at the National Theatre of Ghana. She and groups of singers have traveled to Ghana to study drumming and dance and presented concert tours in Rome, Fossano and Florence, Italy as well as Honolulu, Hawaii. She is a recipient of the Montgomery County Arts and Cultural District Individual Artist Fellowship Award in the Master Artist area.

Rev. Cox is a member of Omega Baptist Church where she and her husband have led the Marriage Builders Ministry for nearly fifteen years. Rev. Cox has a passion for building strong families through ministry to couples, women and young professionals. Her book, *Angels Encamped About Me: Provision In the Wilderness*, was released in September 2007. She is ordained by the American Baptist Churches USA.

Other books by Rev. Dr. Donna Cox
Gospel Songs Your Choir Will Love To Sing (2006, PBM Press)
Music In The Core Curriculum: An Integrative Approach (2000, Euridition)
African American Women Music Professors Singing The Blues (Chapter)
      in *Black Women In The Academy: Promises and Perils*

Sample Workshops & Marriage Retreats
✝ Every Marriage Is A Fixer-Upper
✝ Touch Up Your Roots: Growing A Strong Marriage
✝ The Marriage Dance
✝ More Than You and Me: Touching Others With Your Marriage
✝ The Five Love Languages
✝ Love and Respect: Applying God's Word In A Way That Makes Sense
✝ Why We Act The Way We Do
✝ Conflict That Connects
✝ Raising Godly Children
✝ Honoring Your Covenant
✝ Having A Mary Heart In A Martha World
✝ What To Do When You Don't Know What To Do
✝ The Postures of Praise
✝ Angels Encamped About Me
✝ No More Suicide: Changing The Words You Speak
✝ Sabbath Rest Retreats for Busy Women Who Need A Break™
✝ 24-30 Somethings: The 'What Now' Generation
✝ It's All About You: Preparing Yourself To Be The Best Mate
✝ Breaking Ungodly Soul Ties

Dr. Cox will tailor workshops or retreats to meet the specific needs of your group or congregation. Her style is interactive and engaging.

"We deeply appreciate the balance of humor and practical application which [Rev. Cox] exhibited in facilitating the retreat." Rev. Dr. McKinney, pastor

"[Rev. Cox has] a wonderful way of keeping it real and making the scripture come alive. Thanks!" Karen

"After the retreat, I felt like a huge weight had been lifted from my soul." Marcia

www.ingramcontent.com/pod-product-compliance
Lightning Source LLC
Chambersburg PA
CBHW020915090426
42736CB00008B/639